ONLINE BUSINESS CLASSES

MASTERING MARKETING STRATEGIES TO BUILD AND GROW YOUR ONLINE BUSINESS

BY

MELISSA M. BACKES

COPYRIGHT

DISCLAIMER

ABOUT THE AUTHOR

Melissa M. Backes is dedicated to empowering entrepreneurs in establishing and expanding their online ventures. With a keen interest in the digital landscape, [Melissa M. Backes] brings a wealth of knowledge and experience to help individuals navigate the complexities of online business development

.

Melissa M. Backes expertise lies in:

Business Strategy Development: Crafting effective strategies tailored to the online business landscape.
Entrepreneurial Mentorship: Guiding aspiring entrepreneurs through the challenges of starting and scaling online ventures.
Digital Marketing Insights: Leveraging digital marketing tools and techniques for business growth.
E-commerce Optimization: Streamlining e-commerce operations and enhancing profitability.
Innovative Solutions: Implementing innovative approaches to stay competitive in the online market.

Mission:
Melissa M. Backes is passionate about:

Empowering entrepreneurs with actionable insights and strategies.
Enabling individuals to navigate the dynamic online business environment confidently.
Sharing expertise and proven methodologies to foster business success in the digital realm.

Vision:
Melissa M. Backes envisions a future where:

Entrepreneurial dreams are nurtured into successful online enterprises.
Businesses thrive by leveraging digital advancements and strategic insights.
Collaboration and mentorship drive sustainable growth and innovation in the online business sphere.

Commitment:
With a commitment to excellence and a deep-rooted passion for supporting entrepreneurial endeavors, Melissa M. Backes endeavors to:

Continuously share valuable content, resources, and guides for aspiring and established business owners.
Provide actionable strategies and insights to navigate the evolving online business landscape.
Foster a community of learning and growth for entrepreneurs seeking to build and expand their online presence.

TABLE OF CONTENT

CHAPTER 1

INTRODUCTION

In the quickly developing universe of business, the web-based climate has turned into the focal point of pioneering development. The computerized scene offers a wealth of chances and difficulties that business people and business pioneers should explore to lay out and develop their web-based ventures. This part fills in as the fundamental venturing stone for your excursion into the many-sided universe of online business. In this debut section, we leave on an excursion into the powerful domain of online business, where potential open doors and difficulties proliferate. This section is your door to fathoming the complex scene of advanced business, establishing the groundwork for your endeavor's prosperity.

Grasping the Computerized Business Environment

Grasping the computerized business environment involves a mindset shift towards leveraging technology, data-driven insights and ethical practices to navigate the dynamic and rapidly evolving digital marketplace. It's about embracing innovation, adapting to change and leveraging the vast opportunities offered by the digital world to drive business success. In this part, we dig into the intricacies of the computerized business environment. We investigate the central members, from web based business goliaths to troublesome new companies, and inspect how the serious scene is continually evolving. You'll acquire bits of knowledge into the elements that drive the web-based market, understanding how different components interconnect. This segment uncovers the complicated interchange of parts inside the computerized business biological system. Dive into an extensive investigation of key members, going from industry titans to imaginative new companies. Acquire knowledge into the consistently advancing serious scene, revealing insight into the perplexing trap of associations that shape the internet based market.

Latest Things and Market Elements

Effective internet based organizations stay sensitive to the always moving business sector patterns. We investigate the most recent patterns that are molding the advanced business scene, from the ascent of portable trade to the effect of virtual entertainment on buyer conduct. This part outfits you with the information expected to adjust and flourish in a quickly evolving commercial center. In the journey for progress, remaining informed about advancing business sector elements is principal. This portion takes apart the most recent patterns impacting the computerized business field. From the unavoidable impact of versatile trade to the significant effect of virtual entertainment on buyer conduct, you'll foster an intense attention to the powers driving change in the advanced commercial center.

Distinguishing Valuable open doors for Development

Business visionaries frequently find amazing learning experiences concealed inside market holes. We talk about techniques for distinguishing undiscovered specialties and underexplored market fragments. Toward the finish of this section, you'll be prepared to leave on your web-based business venture with a reasonable comprehension of the scene and the potential. A focal topic in web-based business is the specialty of spotting stowed open doors inside the market scene. Here, we give systems to perceiving unknown specialties and undiscovered market fragments. By the part's end, you will have the sharpness to set out on your internet based business venture with an insightful eye, prepared to recognize and hold onto the potential for significant development.

This part lays the preparation for the astonishing and now and again erratic universe of online business. Furnished with information about the computerized environment, current market elements, and the quest for useful learning experiences, you'll be more ready to settle on informed choices and diagram a fruitful course for your internet based undertaking. This part fills in as your underlying submersion into the powerful universe of online business. Furnished with experiences into the advanced environment, a consciousness of winning business sector elements, and the capacity to distinguish amazing open doors for extension, you are ready to settle on educated choices and explore the intricacies regarding your internet based business attempt successfully.

CHAPTER 2

DEFINING YOUR NICHE AND VALUE PROPOSITION

In this part, we will jump profound into the core of your web-based business. Characterizing your specialty and making a one of a kind incentive are basic to your prosperity. How about we investigate these critical components?

Leading Inside and out Statistical surveying

Understanding your market resembles finding the fortune guide to progress. We'll direct you through the method involved with leading exhaustive statistical surveying. This includes breaking down your main interest group, concentrating on your rivals, and recognizing patterns and holes on the lookout. Furnished with this information, you'll be more ready to make key decisions.Market research is the most common way of social event, investigating, and deciphering information about a specific market, including its buyers, rivals, and patterns. With regards to online business, directing top to bottom statistical surveying is fundamental for pursuing informed choices and setting a strong starting point for your endeavor. Here is a more definite clarification of this vital stage:

1: Grasping Your Ideal interest group: Your most memorable center is to get to know pretty much everything there is to know about your likely clients. This includes making point by point client personas or profiles. You'll need to comprehend their socioeconomics, conduct, inclinations, problem areas, and purchasing propensities. This information will assist you with fitting your items or administrations to really address their issues.

2:Studying Your Rivals: Examining your rivals is a basic part of statistical surveying. You'll need to distinguish who your immediate and roundabout contenders are. Concentrate on their assets and shortcomings, their promoting systems, and their client base. This data can assist you with separating your business and track down ways of beating your rivals.

3:Market Patterns and Holes: Watch out for market drifts and rising amazing open doors. This could include concentrating on industry reports, going to applicable meetings, and keeping awake to-date with industry distributions. Recognize holes in the market that your business can fill, or patterns that you can use for your potential benefit.

4:Customer Studies and Input: Drawing in with your potential clients straightforwardly through overviews, meetings, or criticism structures can give important bits of knowledge. Get some information about their trouble spots, what they esteem in an item or administration, and what upgrades they might want to see. This immediate criticism can be important for fitting your contributions.

5: Online apparatuses and Examination: Use online devices like Google Investigation, web-based entertainment experiences, and watchword research instruments to accumulate information on internet based purchaser conduct. This information can assist you with understanding how individuals find your site, what they do once they're there, and what content or items are generally well known.

6: Testing and Approval: Make it a point to limited scope tests or experimental runs projects to approve your thoughts. For example, you can make greeting pages to measure interest in an item or administration before completely sending it off. Testing permits you to accumulate genuine information and make changes prior to increasing.

7:Data Examination and Understanding: Gathering information is just a portion of the fight. You really want to investigate the information you've gathered and decipher it to make significant determinations. This could include searching for examples, patterns, or connections that can direct your navigation.

Recognizing a Productive Specialty

Recognizing a productive specialty is tied in with figuring out that perfect balance in the market where you can flourish. It's not just about picking something you're keen on; it's tied in with finding a space where there's interest and opportunity. Here is a more top to bottom glance at how to go about it:

Enthusiasm and information are the foundation of any effective undertaking. We should dig further into how they assume an essential part in recognizing a beneficial specialty for your web-based business:

Energy and Information

1. Energy: Your enthusiasm resembles the fuel that keeps your innovative motor running. At the point when you're energetic about something, you're bound to remain committed, in any event, when confronted with difficulties. This is the way energy becomes possibly the most important factor:

Supported Responsibility: Your energy for a specific region makes it simpler to remain committed and steady. Building a business takes time and exertion, and your energy will be the main impetus that makes all the difference for you.

Inventive Critical thinking: When you're enthusiastic about a specialty, you're bound to think imaginatively and concoct creative arrangements. Your energy can prompt new thoughts and one of a kind methodologies that put you aside.

Pleasure and Satisfaction: Building a business is an excursion that can require quite a long while. In the event that you're energetic about what you do, it won't feel like a task. All things considered, it turns into a wellspring of delight and individual satisfaction.

2. Information: While energy gives inspiration, information furnishes you with the devices to effectively explore your picked specialty. This is the way information becomes possibly the most important factor:

Skill: Your current information and mastery in a specific field can give you an upper hand. It permits you to give an elevated degree of significant worth to your clients, making them bound to pick your items or administrations.

Risk Relief: When you have a profound comprehension of a specialty, you can go with additional educated choices. This information assists you with expecting difficulties, alleviating gambles, and adjusting to changes on the lookout.

Building Believability: Information breeds validity. At the point when you can show your mastery inside a specialty, it constructs trust with your crowd. Clients are bound to trust and purchase from organizations that plainly grasp their requirements.

Content Creation: On the off chance that you have information in a specialty, you can make important substance that teaches and connects with your crowd. Content showcasing is an incredible asset for online organizations, and your insight can be the wellspring of educational and important substance.

It's critical to find some kind of harmony between your energy and information while recognizing a beneficial specialty. Your energy energizes your drive, however your insight gives the course. In a perfect world, your picked specialty ought to line up with both your enthusiasm and your mastery. This arrangement makes the excursion more pleasant as well as expands your odds of coming out on top, as you can use your energy and information to hang out on the lookout.

3: Market Interest: Exploration the market to check whether there's an interest for your picked specialty. Search for indications of interest, like inquiry volume, online entertainment conversations, or the presence of contenders. A specialty with a current client base is a decent sign.

Market request is a basic component while picking a specialty for your web-based business. It basically responds to the inquiry: Are there individuals able to purchase what you're presenting in your picked specialty? Here is a more intensive glance at market interest and what it means for your specialty determination:

a:Customer Need and Want: The groundwork of market requests lies in the requirements and wants of your possible clients. To evaluate this:

Distinguish Trouble spots: Consider the issues or problem areas your ideal interest group faces. What are they searching for answers for? Specialty regions with major problems will quite often have more popularity for arrangements.

Evaluate Wants and Interests: Comprehend what your interest group wants or is keen on. Individuals are bound to spend on things they are energetic about or profoundly keen on.

b:Research and Information Examination: To measure market request successfully:

Watchword Exploration: Use devices like Google Catchphrase Organizer or other Web optimization instruments to recognize the quest volume for explicit catch phrases connected with your specialty. Higher pursuit volumes frequently demonstrate more popularity.

Web-based Entertainment Patterns: Screen online entertainment stages and gatherings connected with your specialty. Search for conversations, remarks, and offers. High commitment to these spaces can be an indication of interest.

c: Contender Investigation: Dissecting your rivals can give bits of knowledge into market interest:

Contender Achievement: In the event that there are effective organizations in your picked specialty, a pointer there's a market able to spend. Concentrate on these contenders to find out about their procedures.

d: Interest group Approval: To guarantee that your ideal interest group is keen on your specialty:

Studies and Input: Draw in with your likely clients through reviews or criticism structures to get some information about their necessities and interests straightforwardly. This may provide important tidbits of information.

e:Patterns and Market Advancement: Assess the drawn out practicality of your specialty by thinking about how it might develop and adjust to changing business sector patterns.

f:. Administrative and Lawful Contemplations:

Consistence: Guarantee that you get it and record for any lawful or administrative prerequisites inside your specialty, which might influence your expenses and productivity.

Productivity evaluation is fundamental since it assists you with checking whether your picked specialty can support a beneficial business. It guarantees that your internet based business can produce pay that covers your costs as well as considers development and, eventually, achievement. While enthusiasm and interest in a specialty are significant, they should be offset with a reasonable evaluation of its productivity to make informed

5: Long haul Reasonability

Long haul reasonability is a basic component while choosing a specialty for your web-based business. It includes evaluating whether your picked specialty can endure everyday hardship and keep on offering amazing open doors for development and achievement. Here is a more nitty gritty investigation of how to assess the drawn out practicality of a specialty:

1. Manageable Patterns and Market Advancement:

Market Patterns: Assess the patterns molding your picked specialty. Maintainable patterns show soundness and long haul interest. Consider whether these patterns line up with the developing necessities and inclinations of your interest group.

Versatility: Survey the flexibility of your specialty to changes in innovation, shopper conduct, and market elements. Specialties that can advance and embrace developments are bound to be suitable over the long haul.

2. Client Conduct and Socioeconomics:

Evolving Socio Economics: Consider whether the socioeconomics of your ideal interest group are probably going to change over the long run. A specialty that takes care of a steady or developing segment is by and large more feasible in the long haul.

Changes in Purchaser Conduct: Dissect likely changes in shopper conduct inside your specialty. Understanding how your crowd could change their inclinations or assumptions can assist you with adjusting your business methodologies appropriately.

3. Administrative Security:

Legitimate and Administrative Climate: Analyze the lawful and administrative climate applicable to your specialty. Specialties that work inside a steady and unsurprising administrative structure are for the most part more feasible in the long haul.

Expectation of Changes: Remain informed about any possible changes in guidelines that could affect your specialty. Being proactive in adjusting to administrative changes can improve long haul feasibility.

4. Innovation and Industry Headways:

Innovation Coordination: Survey how your specialty incorporates propelling advances. Specialties that hug and adjust to innovative headways are bound to stay important and reasonable.

Industry Advancement: Think about the degree of development inside your specialty. Businesses that persistently advance are better situated for long haul achievement.

5. Monetary Resilience:Economic Elements: Assess what financial circumstances might mean for your specialty. Specialties that exhibit strength during financial slumps or vulnerabilities are bound to be suitable in the long haul.

Enhancement Systems: Investigate techniques to broaden your contributions or income streams inside the specialty. Broadening can improve your capacity to climate financial difficulties.

6. Rivalry Elements:

Serious Scene: Screen the cutthroat scene inside your specialty. Specialties with sound rivalry and the potential for new contestants are bound to stay lively in the long haul.

Development and Separation: Endeavor to enhance and separate your contributions consistently. This assists you with standing apart as well as adds to the drawn out manageability of your business inside the specialty.

7. Social and Ecological Contemplations:

Social Patterns: Consider what social patterns might mean for your specialty. Specialties that line up with positive social qualities or natural manageability are many times more interesting to shoppers over the long haul.

Ecological Effect: Survey the natural effect of your specialty. Organizations that focus on manageability are probably going to be stronger in a socially cognizant market.

Creating A One of a kind Incentive

Making a special incentive is likened to creating a charming story that brings your crowd into the narrative of your business. How about we dive into the human imaginativeness behind this cycle:

Understanding Client Needs: Start by venturing into the shoes of your clients. What difficulties do they face, and what wants fuel their decisions? A convincing incentive tends to these requirements, reverberating with the desires and trouble spots of your crowd.

Lucidity and Straightforwardness: Envision your incentive as a reasonable, brief story that anybody can comprehend. Stay away from language and intricacy. Effortlessness is the brushstroke that illustrates what separates your business.

Center around Advantages, Not Elements: Consider your item or administration highlights as characters in your story. Nonetheless, the account's quintessence lies in the advantages these highlights bring to your clients. Feature how your contribution works on their lives or tackles their concerns.

Extraordinary Selling Suggestion (USP): Your USP is the hero of your business story. What makes your business the legend according to your clients? Recognize this novel perspective — be it a particular component, unrivaled quality, or uncommon help — and mesh it into your incentive.

Profound Association: People interface with feelings. Inject your incentive with feeling, making a reverberation that goes past simple value-based requests. Whether it's satisfaction, security, or comfort, summon feelings that wait in the hearts of your crowd.

Separation in a Packed Space: Picture your business as a person in a jam-packed market show. How does your personality stick out? Make an incentive that features your particular characteristics, making a critical person in the packed story of your specialty.

Communicate in Your Client's Language: Envision your offer as a discussion between companions. Use language that your clients get and connect with. This association constructs trust and guarantees that your message resounds genuinely.

Visual Narrating: People are visual animals. Upgrade your incentive with visual components — a convincing logo, symbolism, or even a video — that adds a visual layer to your story. These visuals ought to line up with the feelings and informing of your incentive.

Consistency Across Touchpoints: Imagine your incentive as a steady topic going through each section of your business story. Whether on your site, virtual entertainment, or client corporations, keep a durable story that builds up your extraordinary worth.

Persistent Refinement: Envision your incentive as a no nonsense content. Routinely return to and refine it. The business scene develops, and your incentive ought to adjust likewise, remaining important and full.

Client Tributes as Story Supports: Consider your fulfilled clients characters who vouch for the credibility of your account. Integrate client tributes as strong supports that add validity and build up the special worth your business conveys.

CHAPTER 3: BUILDING AREAS OF STRENGTH FOR A PRESENCE

Like structure a realm, constructing a web-based presence requires exertion, time and cash. Not exclusively will you really want to have some place for clients to land (for example a site), yet you'll likewise have to make various pathways to lead them there and persuade them that your business merits their time. So how would you make it happen?

The key to having areas of strength for a presence is to appear on a few critical sorts of stages and make positive and reliable commitments. As your crowd sees your commitment on the web, they are bound to consider you a dependable, trustworthy and — in particular — real business

Making an Expert Site and Portable Improvement

Construct a Site

 Your business site is your on the web "home" — where you characterize your business, impart your qualities, exhibit your items and welcome possible clients. Each of your other web-based feeds ought to lead individuals back to your site, where you will welcome them to join your prizes program, buy into messages or make a buy.

There are a few choices for building a site that likewise works as a web-based store. For instance, you can:

Construct a site and coordinate an installment entryway through a fitting and-play Programming interface module that accompanies a trader record and shipper administrations

Construct a site utilizing a fledgling's foundation like Wix that accompanies discretionary web-based store offices

Fabricate your site utilizing a devoted shopping stage like Shopify or BigCommerce

Whichever choice you pick, your site ought to be not difficult to explore, have wonderful, proficient item pictures and have clear source of inspiration buttons like "join" and "purchase now". Incorporate trust identifications to show that you use extortion counteraction apparatuses and social verification like client tributes and surveys.

List Your Items in Web-based Commercial centers

When you have a web-based store, recall that you can likewise sell your items on uber markets like Amazon, eBay, Google Shopping, Alibaba and Etsy. Numerous clients start their item look through straightforwardly in Amazon or Google Shopping. Having postings there will assist them with tracking down you.

While selling through uber markets, for example, the ones referenced above, make certain to give a connection back to your site in the item depiction. In the event that the client is content with their buy, they could come straightforwardly to your site to buy sometime later — bringing about higher net revenues on ensuing deals.

Remember Your Image for Online Indexes

On the off chance that you're a neighborhood business, online indexes are a significant device for helping your internet based presence. It's even conceivable that postings have been made for you, however may be erroneous or inadequate.

At the very least, guarantee your business on Google My Business (GMB) and add a short business depiction and a connection to your site. Then, at that point, make postings for the top indexes for your locale. For Europe, consider:

Europages

Eurobiz Online

UK Independent venture Catalog

Europe Professional reference On the web

When your business is recorded, try to keep your location, contact subtleties and site URL exceptional. This is significant for client trust and validity.

Construct Your Standing through Web-based Surveys

Buyers depend intensely on web-based surveys for coming to conclusions about a buy. As a matter of fact, 95% of clients read surveys online before they even go into a store. While a few potential clients will peruse surveys unpredictably, others search for audits from the previous month as they comprehend this surrenders the most to-date image of your momentum item quality and client assistance.

As well as requesting that clients leave tributes, evaluations and surveys on your site, it's really smart to welcome clients to leave audits on outsider locales like Google Audits. In the two cases, ensure you answer client criticism and surveys (both positive and negative) to show that you're checking criticism and really care about your clients.

Compose Visitor Posts for Significant position Web journals

Visitor posting is an incredible method for expanding the perceivability of your internet based business through the making of backlinks to your webpage. Search for famous web journals in your specialty and try out pertinent substance thoughts to the supervisor. Some of the time you'll have to pay for the post (alluded to as a "supported article") and different times they'll incorporate endorsed articles free of charge.

To help your site significantly more, attempt to get backlinks to your site from significant position spaces like news locales and those consummation in .edu and .gov. The most ideal way to do this is to direct unique examination and market reviews and distribute the outcomes.

Make a Wikipedia Passage

This methodology is generally pertinent to establishments and people, yet making a Wikipedia passage helps your apparent power — in the event that you're on Wikipedia, you should be somebody. All you want to do to compose a Wikipedia passage about your business is make a record, give your essential data and compose intriguing realities about your organization's set of experiences and accomplishments.

Assuming you choose to show up on Wikipedia, it's critical to give significant position sources to your data, remain objective (not self-advancing) and tell the truth in the event that there have been any discussions in your organization's set of experiences. It's greatly improved to be direct and show how you've improved as opposed to hang tight for another person to uncover your weaknesses.

Open Web-based Entertainment Records

A web-based entertainment presence is an extraordinary method for building brand mindfulness and interface with your crowd in a more cheerful manner. Via virtual entertainment, you'll regularly post fun, short, character filled posts, eye-getting pictures, recordings, contests and deals. Your clients can collaborate with you in a more casual environment, furnish criticism and offer with their companions.

To start, you'll have to foster a virtual entertainment system that recognizes:

The virtual entertainment stages that your ideal interest group utilizes (like Facebook, Instagram, YouTube, Twitter, Snapchat, TikTok and Pinterest)

The days and times your ideal interest group is probably going to be on the web

The sorts of posts that are the best for every virtual entertainment stage

In the event that you're utilizing Facebook, for instance, you'll need to utilize a blend of:

33% of presents that relate straightforwardly on your items and advancements

33% of posts that share industry bits of knowledge and insights

33% of posts that welcome crowd cooperation and input

Assuming you're utilizing different stages, figure out which methodologies work best. For instance, Stories will generally work best on Instagram and short demonstrational recordings function admirably on YouTube. Facebook local recordings work better compared to connections to YouTube and square pictures give you more visual land contrasted with square shapes.

While utilizing virtual entertainment to construct your internet based presence, it's critical to present routinely and answer on remarks and messages. You can make a substance schedule for each impending month to ensure you have a decent blend of profoundly captivating substance types.

On the off chance that you're a neighborhood business, online catalogs are a significant instrument for supporting your internet based presence. It's even conceivable that postings have been made for you, yet may be mistaken or fragmented.At least, guarantee your business on Google My Business (GMB) and add a short business depiction and a connection to your site. Then, at that point, make postings for the top indexes for your area.

Fostering a Compelling Substance Technique

Whenever you've made your site and virtual entertainment profiles, composed a Wikipedia section (if pertinent) and are recorded on the significant catalogs, all that is passed on to do is help your pages and business with showcasing. There are a few computerized promoting techniques you ought to use notwithstanding paid showcasing to push your postings higher on the SERPs.

Content Advertising

Content advertising includes making watchword enhanced content to show web indexes the significance of your site to clients. Catchphrases are the word coordinates and expressions that web clients enter in a Bing or Google search. By matching your substance near these expressions and inquiries, your site is bound to make it onto the outcomes list.

Regardless, you'll need to make your site web search tool amicable with site improvement (Web optimization). Perform watchword research and remember the important catchphrases for your URLs, meta-information, titles, headings, record names and alt labels. Then, at that point, begin making content consistently as blog articles and recordings. The more applicable articles you have, the more open doors there will be for intrigued clients to track down your site.

Powerhouse Promoting

Powerhouse showcasing depicts joint efforts among organizations and online VIPs in which the famous people (otherwise known as forces to be reckoned with) elevate your items to their crowd. This is a digit like the old arrangement of supports, then again, actually these aren't conventional competitors or pop stars — they're independent virtual entertainment VIPs with an exceptionally evolved specialty.

To advance your items with powerhouse showcasing, track down forces to be reckoned with in your locale and specialty and move toward them to see whether your items may bear some significance with their crowd. Then, give your site address and online entertainment handles so that the force to be reckoned with can connect to you in their posts.

Paid Promoting

Paid web based publicizing ought not be your just or essentially even a drawn out methodology, however it can go far to supporting your perceivability while you work on your natural rankings.

Google, Bing and Hurray all have pay-per-click publicizing programs, and that implies that you possibly pay when somebody taps on the promotion. At the point when you pursue Google Promotions, you'll gain admittance to find out about AdWords, which can be an incredible wellspring of watchword research for your substance showcasing too.

Via online entertainment, you're taking a gander at paid promotions that are typically evaluated by the recurrence and reach of the promotion. Online entertainment advertisements ought to constantly accompany an eye-getting "inspire" button that takes clients to your principal business site.

RICH Pieces, Included Bits, RELATED Inquiries AND Connections

You have an extraordinary site, great substance, a solid online entertainment presence and many positive surveys. Presently, unite everything with methodologies that show your prosperity to the world.

Rich Bits

On each page of your site — particularly top-selling items pages — add pattern markup to tell web search tools where to find the item name, item picture, value, evaluations and stock accessibility on the page. This data will show to intrigued clients, assisting them with contrasting comparable items without having with click into every site. They can then go to your site with a firm aim to purchase.

Highlighted Bits

Highlighted bits show at the highest point of Google query items (for nothing) and give compact solutions to questions that web clients inquire. To be chosen for included scraps, attempt to give exceptionally applicable proclamations close to the highest point of each article. For instance, in an inside plan article about red versus blue for walls, incorporate a sentence like: "red walls make a sensation of warmth though blue walls make a sensation of quiet".

Related Inquiries

Google's "kin additionally inquired" or "related questions" is driven by calculations that examine subheadings (H2s) in blog entries. You have a higher possibility of being highlighted in the event that you structure your H2s as questions and answer a few related inquiries in each post.

Joins

Interior and outside joins in posts show web crawlers which pages are connected and which ones are viewed as the most important. The more connections that lead to a given objective page, the higher its doled out score. You can build the perceivability of two pages immediately by incorporating interior connections with anchor text that is important both to the source and target page.

BUILDING Major areas of strength for a PRESENCE CAN DO Miracles FOR YOUR Image

Laying out and keeping a simple to-explore site, running influencing virtual entertainment missions and staying up with the latest takes work, yet will assist you with building serious areas of strength for a presence and lift your believability with clients.

To get everything rolling, direct statistical surveying, foster a triumphant methodology and collaborate with people and organizations who can assist with executing your thoughts. Being steady with content creation and showing clients that you care about their experience (by answering remarks and audits) won't just work on your perceivability however reinforce your standing also.

Utilizing Web-based Entertainment for Brand Perceivability

In the present advanced age, online entertainment has turned into an essential device for organizations to improve their image presence and associate with their ideal interest group. Utilizing virtual entertainment stages actually can altogether affect brand perceivability, client commitment, and, eventually, business achievement. This article investigates the prescribed procedures for utilizing online entertainment for the end goal of marking and gives genuine contextual analyses that exhibit the fruitful execution of these techniques.

Understanding Virtual Entertainment Marking

To use virtual entertainment actually for marking, it is pivotal to comprehend its importance in the cutting edge promoting scene. Virtual entertainment stages offer a tremendous crowd base and give organizations a valuable chance to construct areas of strength for a picture. Marking via virtual entertainment includes making a reliable brand voice, visual character, and narrating across various stages. It additionally involves drawing in with the crowd, cultivating brand reliability, and driving changes.

Best Practices for Virtual Entertainment Marking

Characterize your image personality: Prior to jumping into web-based entertainment marking, organizations should have a reasonable comprehension of their image character, values, and interest group. This information will direct the formation of content that reverberates with the target group and lines up with the brand's general picture.

Steady brand informing

to web-based entertainment marking. Keep a consistent brand voice, tone, and visual personality across all web-based entertainment channels. This guarantees that clients can undoubtedly perceive and connect with your image, no matter what the stage they experience it on.

Tailor content to every stage

Different virtual entertainment stages have particular qualities and client inclinations. Tailor your substance to suit every stage's arrangement, crowd assumptions, and commitment designs. This could include adjusting visuals, utilizing applicable hashtags, and using stage explicit elements like Stories or live recordings.

Connect with and communicate

Online entertainment is a two-way correspondence channel.Engage with your audience by answering remarks, messages, and notices. Empower conversations, clarify pressing issues, and look for input. Building associations with your crowd encourages brand steadfastness and makes a positive brand picture.

CHAPTER 4 :ONLINE BUSINESS GREATNESS

In the flourishing scene of web based shopping, making an online business site that draws in guests as well as converts them into clients is a mind boggling workmanship. The opposition is savage, and the customers are requesting. How might you plan an internet business stage that stands apart from the group and prompts transformation?

In this complete aide, we will dig into the core of online business plan methodologies that drive transformation. From understanding client conduct to executing dependable plan strategies, we'll investigate all that you really want to be aware of to transform easygoing guests into steadfast clients.

Setting up and dealing with an Online business stage

Instructions to set up Internet business site

Stage 1. Pick your substance the board framework (CMS)

The groundwork of each and every site is a substance of the board framework (CMS). There are various different substance the executives frameworks to browse open-source stages, for example, WordPress to novice well disposed across the board web designers like Shopify or Squarespace. Which is appropriate for yourself as well as your web-based store will rely upon your financial plan, insight, and one of a kind online business needs.

Here are the most well known content administration frameworks for online business sites:

WordPress: The world's driving CMS that is additionally one of the most customisable.

Stage 6. Set up an installment door, stock and duty instruments

After you have populated your online business site, there are a couple of key parts of building an online business webpage to take care of from setting up an installment processor to adding stock and duty devices.

Pick an installment entryway

With regards to picking and setting up an installment entryway, numerous internet based retailers settle on outsider devices, for example, Stripe or PayPal to make the cycle simpler and safer. Assuming you are diverting the client to different sites, you should guarantee that the information is completely encoded before move.

In the event that you are picking installment reconciliations, think about these focuses:

How simple is it to incorporate the instrument with your foundation?

Is the instrument secure?

Is the instrument PCI agreeable?

What are the charges you and the client should pay?

For a nitty gritty breakdown, allude to our article on the best installment entryways.

Incorporate transportation

On the off chance that your foundation permits it, you ought to incorporate transportation with your web based business site for a consistent encounter. It will likewise improve on activities and you can zero in on selling. Be that as it may, before you incorporate transportation, decide your delivery approaches like free delivery, variable expense, level rate, and so on. And keeping in mind that you are busy, likewise lay out discount and merchandise exchanges.

Add a deals charge mini-computer (discretionary)

Moreover, you might need to consider adding a duty number cruncher to compute Tank, delivery and some other charges at checkout consequently.

Stage 7. Test and send off your web based business website

Prior to sending off the web based business website to your clients, you should check the website completely. Each button and each connection on the site should work. Indeed, even 404 mistake pages ought to be planned by the subject.

Run tests to check whether you can add items to the truck and interaction the installment. Most stages will permit you to test installment handling without really charging your Visa.

Make certain to browse on the off chance that every one of the messages are getting shipped off the right inboxes after a buy has been made or declined. Also, to wrap things up, check how your site looks and works on cell phones. If conceivable, attempt to look at the website's exhibition on various internet browsers.

Whenever you have tried and twofold really look at everything, from item depictions to class pages, you are prepared to send off.

Report the send off of your web based business store through your virtual entertainment pages, visitor posts on well known retail writes in your specialty, powerhouse advertising and to your email records. On the off chance that you have the financial plan, you can likewise go for paid promotion on Facebook, Google and different stages.

Advantages of selling on the web

Before you really begin constructing your internet business site, you should be clear about your business needs for building a site. Here are a few motivations behind why you ought to sell on the web.

More purchasers are going on the web

Purchasing on the web is helpful as well as protected, and during the pandemic, web based business deals flooded by as much as 40% in 2020, the principal pandemic year. The simple accessibility of cell phones additionally implies that you can purchase from anyplace, any time. So clearly individuals will keep purchasing long after the pandemic has lessened.

Setting up an online business shopfront is less expensive

Advancing Transformation Rates and Client Experience

The objective of transformation rate enhancement is to further develop the client experience and urge guests to make the ideal move, like making a buy or finishing up a structure. Web composition, route, content, speed, and personalization all play

With regards to changing over site guests into clients, the client experience is everything. A consistent, natural, and charming experience can have a significant effect on whether a guest chooses to make the following stride and make a purchase. Then again, a disappointing, confounding, or generally upsetting experience can drive potential clients away, leaving you with a low transformation rate and botched open doors. In this article, we'll investigate why client experience is a particularly basic figure change rate enhancement, and how you can utilize it to help your primary concern. In this way, assuming that you're hoping to advance your site and increment transformations, continue to peruse!

Understanding the association between client experience and transformation rate

With regards to site enhancement, it's essential to comprehend the association between client experience and transformation rate. Basically, client experience alludes to the general feel and nature of a site according to a guest's point of view. It envelops everything from web architecture and route, to the speed and usefulness of the webpage. Then again, transformation rate alludes to the level of site guests who make an ideal move, like making a buy or finishing up a structure.

The association between client experience and transformation rate is basic: a positive client experience prompts higher change rates, while a negative client experience prompts lower change rates. This is on the grounds that a site that offers a consistent, natural, and pleasant experience is bound to keep guests drew in and urge them to make the following stride and make a buy. Then again, a site that is baffling, confounding, or generally unsavory is bound to drive guests away, bringing about a low exchange rate.

In this way, assuming that you're hoping to improve your site and increment transformations, it's crucial for center around upgrading the client experience. By making a site that is not difficult to utilize, quick, and charming, you'll keep guests drawn in, yet in addition increase the possibilities of them making the ideal move and supporting your change rate.

The effect of web composition on client experience and changes

Web composition assumes an immense part in deciding the client experience and at last, the change rate. A very much planned site looks great, yet additionally gives a consistent and instinctive experience for guests. Then again, an ineffectively planned site can be confusing, baffling, and drive guests away.

A vital part of web composition that influences client experience is the design and association of the website. A spotless and coordinated design makes it simple for guests to find what they are searching for, while a jumbled and complicated format can be confounding and overpowering. Furthermore, the utilization of variety, typography, and pictures can likewise incredibly influence the client experience. The right blend of these components can make an outwardly engaging and drawing experience, while some unacceptable mix can reduce the general feel of the site.

One more significant part of web architecture that influences client experience is the responsiveness of the website. A site that is streamlined for cell phones gives a superior encounter to guests who are utilizing their cell phones or tablets to get to the site. Then again, a site that isn't upgraded for cell phones can be slow and challenging to explore, bringing about a negative client experience.

All in all, client experience is a basic consideration of transformation rate enhancement. By zeroing in on web architecture, route, content, speed, personalization, and persistent improvement, you can give the most ideal experience to guests and drive changes.

At the point when you contrast it and a physical store, Setting up an online business retail facade is a lot less expensive. This is somewhat on the grounds that physical stores cause different fixed expenses, for example, lease, power bills, worker installments, foundation upkeep, and so on.

Online business site can help disconnected deals

It isn't required that on the web and disconnected stores ought to be fundamentally unrelated. They can expand each other pleasantly when you educate individuals regarding your physical store on your web based business site and introduce application stands in your stores.

Begin selling right away

When you have the site prepared, everything you really want to do is set up installment handling and rundown your items on the site to begin selling. There is a compelling reason to hang tight for new workers, store stock or produce sufficient promoting buzz. You are ready to go the second you put your site live.

Compelling Stock Administration and Satisfaction

Stock administration is the center component of maintaining a fruitful internet business. It incorporates monitoring your stock and ensuring you have the right items in the ideal amounts brilliantly.

Compelling stock administration is the backbone of a business in light of multiple factors. It guarantees that client request is met, costs are diminished, and the activity of the business is streamlined and flourishing

Satisfy clients need

In this day and age, a business lives and passes on by the client experience. Terrible client surveys can be a plague and can spread and contaminate would-be clients.

We should investigate the effect of client audits by checking the numbers out. As indicated by Worldwide Newswire, 95% of clients say they read surveys when making a web-based buy. With just 5% of clients not understanding surveys, the effect of each and every unfortunate audit can falter. Consequently, satisfying client needs and giving a positive encounter is a need for a business' prosperity.

Stock administration is a fundamental component to accomplish this. It guarantees that you have the right items accessible when your clients need them - no gem ball required! By precisely anticipating requests and keeping up with ideal stock levels, you can limit those feared stockouts and try not to frustrate your clients. This won't just disperse the plague of terrible surveys, yet it likewise will prompt an expansion in consumer loyalty and reliability.

Lessen costs

Better safe than sorry - and successful stock administration assists you with getting it done. By advancing your stock levels, you can abstain from overloading, which catches important capital and causes extra capacity costs. Then again, stockouts can bring about lost benefits and potential open doors. Find some kind of harmony by keeping stock levels lined up with request, and you can receive the benefits of brought down costs and amplified benefits.

Upgrade income

Stock ties up a lot of working capital. Holding unnecessary stock can strain your income, as it addresses cash that might have been put resources into different regions of your business. By executing productive stock administration rehearsals, you can guarantee that your money isn't pointlessly caught in abundance. For instance, by resolving the issues of under-and over-loading stock, a business can expect about a 10% decrease in stock expenses. That is a significant amount of cash that is ready for venture elsewhere.

Work on functional productivity

Proficient stock administration enables efficiency and intensifies adequacy. By keeping up with exact stock records, no otherworldly spell is expected to find and recover items without any problem. The entire interaction is upgraded in light of the fact that there is a 10,000 foot perspective of everything.

Also, not in the least does a stock administration framework give this outline and understanding, however the going with computerization devices can additionally help efficiency by destroying the requirement for physically following items.

Try not to under-over stock

Under-and overloading can adversely affect an online business. The premonition in the pit of your stomach subsequent to putting in a request and afterward figuring out the item is unavailable should be dodged no matter what. Fortunately, executing stock administration rehearses like interest arranging, setting reorder focuses, and observing stock levels, can assist you with keeping away from this bothersome trap and keep an ideal stock level.

Limit misfortune

The burden of misfortune: Loss of stock altogether affects your primary concern.

Successful stock administration limits misfortune by executing measures to forestall robbery, harm, and deterioration. Standard stock reviews and appropriate stockpiling and taking care of practices can assist with warding off these dangers, guaranteeing that your stock waits - and is productive.

Upgrade request satisfaction

By dealing with your stock actually, you should rest assured that client orders are satisfied quickly and precisely. This at last results in superior request precision, more limited satisfaction times, and less events of delay purchases and replacements. Speedy request satisfaction times likewise improve consumer loyalty. In correlation, research shows that 69% of buyers are less inclined to shop with a retailer later on in the event that a buy isn't conveyed in the span of two days of the guaranteed conveyance

Stock administration frameworks speed up satisfaction times by giving smoothed out request handling, picking, pressing and delivery. Additionally, by coordinating your stock administration framework with your request the executives framework, you can mechanize these cycles, diminish blunders, and further develop request precision. This results in quicker conveyance times, smoother tasks, and more joyful clients.

Acquire an upper hand

In the present online business scene, contests are basically as constant as the grave. Consequently, an upper hand is basic for endurance as well as for development. Dominance over stock can give you that strategic advantage, guaranteeing the right items are available when your rivals face stockouts.

By advancing your stock administration, you can isolate yourself from the shadows of the contest.

Execute a viable stock administration framework

To receive the rewards we have uncovered over, a powerful stock administration framework is the imperative component to development and achievement.

A strong stock administration framework cuts off the chains of rivalry and recognizes your business as the preeminent decision. Outfit mechanization for key cycles like interest anticipating, stock following, request the board, and revealing. Acquire ongoing perceivability into your stock, empowering information driven independent direction and proactive stock administration

CHAPTER 5: ADVANCE PROMOTING DOMINANCE

Defining clear and feasible objectives is fundamental for measuring the viability of your advanced showcasing methodology.

Whether it's rising site traffic, producing leads, or supporting web-based deals, guarantee your objectives are explicit, quantifiable, achievable, pertinent, and time-bound (Savvy).

Distinguish your top business needs and adjust your advanced promoting objectives likewise, like expanding deals, creating leads, or growing brand mindfulness.

High level Search engine optimization Systems and Catchphrase Exploration

What is Progressed Catchphrase Exploration?

Catchphrase research is the method involved with finding and investigating search terms.

Nonetheless, high level watchword examination can assist you with investigating more top to bottom ways of arriving at your Search engine optimization objectives.

Utilizing a high level watchword investigation methodology is one of the main components of cutting edge Search engine optimization on the grounds that occasionally ding deals, creating leads, or growing brand mindfulness.

High level Search engine optimization Systems and Catchphrase fundamental Website design enhancement catchphrase research simply doesn't give the outcomes you're looking for.

We will cover a portion of these terms and techniques to a greater extent later, yet until further notice, we should get reacquainted with a portion of the nuts and bolts:

Search volume: the times that the word or expression is looked for in a particular time frame

Rivalry: measures the number of site pages are focusing on a particular watchword

Trouble: this lets you know the number of different bits of content you that will be rivaling

Watchword hole: gauges the contrast among you and your rival's catchphrase execution

Crowd search expectation: the most common way of grasping the setting of a client's inquiry

Moreover, the following are a couple of cutting edge catchphrase phrases you may not be know all about:

Traffic-creating potential: is a metric that is crucial for cutting edge catchphrase achievement and producing additional natural traffic from your center watchword

Natural snap rate: a metric that shows the number of clients that snap on pages in natural list items for your objective watchword

Google's "kin likewise inquire" watchwords: a segment in Google's query items that presentations questions connected with your pursuit term

Now that we've investigated some fundamental and high level watchword terms and expressions, we should continue on toward cutting edge catchphrase types:

Various Sorts of Cutting edge Watchword Exploration

While making Website design enhancement content that objectives a particular inquiry, you will likewise need to cover a scope of related search questions and pertinent catchphrases that are connected with it.

They incorporate spelling and phrasing varieties of your center term, normal equivalent words, or option scans making progress toward a similar ultimate objective.

Here is a rundown of significant high level watchword research phrases:

- Long-tail catchphrases
- Marked catchphrases
- Question catchphrases
- Shoulder catchphrases
- Moving or occasional watchwords

Long-tail watchwords are longer inquiry questions consisting of a few words with a lower search volume yet a higher change rate.half of search inquiries contain at least 4 words, so lengthy tail watchwords will be vital for your procedure.

Marked watchwords are looked through that incorporate a brand name or organization.

These sorts of catchphrases will be placed when a searcher is searching for a help or item from a particular business

Furthermore, question catchphrases are search questions that are as questions.

These inquiry watchwords cover your fundamental theme and target catchphrase.

On the off chance that you really want a little assistance finding some inquiry catchphrases for your substance, AnswerThePublic is an incredible spot to begin.

Shoulder watchwords are what your objective clients are effectively looking for yet may not be straightforwardly applicable to your item.

They permit you to build your image mindfulness and get more possible clients to the highest point of your deals channel.

Ultimately, moving or occasional catchphrases are well known phrases that are being looked for presently or during a specific season, this can be useful while focusing on satisfied for occasions or moving reports.

High level Search engine optimization Catchphrase Exploration Techniques

Catchphrase research is one of the establishment pieces for Search engine optimization. It has an essential impact in understanding what your interest group is effectively looking for and the sort of happy that is popular.

High level watchword research helps shape your business' compelling and solid Web optimization technique.

All things considered, how about we investigate some high level watchword research techniques you can utilize at the present time:

Use low competition expressions

For certain associations, low challenge expressions are your key to web crawler detectable quality and attract more busy time gridlock to your business.

Low challenge expressions are the chases that probably won't have an unfathomably high watchword search volume, yet critical position regions don't at this point overpower them.

Numerous people expect they can find low-contention expression contemplations by entering their watchword into an investigation gadget and looking at the expression inconvenience bar.

You should then truly investigate the resistance for every articulation by doing a Google search.

If there are under 500 results for a watchword, you can consider it a low challenge.

Coming up next are two or three methods for finding low-competition watchwords:

Use a central objective watchword

See as related or express match watchword considerations

Channel through and look for low-competition expressions

Add channel words, for instance, "buy" or "near me"

Significant level expression research approaches using content openings

Competitor examination should be at the focal point of any general watchword research process, as it gives information into the expressions and backlinks that are working for your top opponents.

You can then sort out what is working for them to make gains for your business.

This is critical as it licenses you to reveal every one of the goal terms that should be centered around in your expression method.

These watchwords should be a truly significant objective in light of the fact that the way that a couple of your opponents rank for them suggests that you can feasibly rank for them also.

Whenever you have recognized these incredible expression openings, you can look at how your opponents have sorted out some way to rank for them.

With this information about blissful and backlinks, you can follow a near method to begin situating for these terms.

Additionally, you can use mechanical assemblies, for instance, Google Search Control focus to help you with tracking down situating open entryways.

The following are a couple of steady thoughts for finding fulfilled openings:

- Contemplate your group's buyer's cycle
- Lead significant factual looking over
- Analyze your past substance for openings
- Analyze any competitors' substance for openings
- Run a substance survey
- Develop your first-page land

This strategy is connected to taking up whatever amount of the chief page on SERPs as could be anticipated.

For sure, even the best watchword doesn't be guaranteed to provoke a #1 situating. Sometimes you just evidently can't move past second, third, or fourth spot.

You might have achieved the essential page, yet that doesn't mean you should give up at this point.

That is where this SERPs dominance methodology comes in!

Accepting your tenacious exertion on your own site has driven you to rank on the essential page for one of your expressions, this moment is the perfect open door to appropriate improved content for that watchword across other power districts.

Critical position areas like YouTube, Medium, and LinkedIn can be by and large used to take up extra spots on the reliably fundamental first page of Google.

For instance, if you at this point have a situating helper on your site for "Expression Investigation Techniques".

You can then convey a YouTube video improved for a comparative key term to get that situation on the essential page too.

Moreover, remember, for help tracking down watchword data for objections with cherishing YouTube, you can use a multi-channel instrument like Soovle.

Explore swarm search reason

Earlier in this article, we discussed the meaning of watchword point and how you can make an interpretation of assumption into 4 social affairs:

Navigational

Informational

Business

Esteem based

This method separates watchwords to sort out the searcher's point, then, uses the results to channel your impressive once-over of expressions into the ones that genuinely matter and the ones that are conceivable an abuse of resources.

For instance, a navigational expression (when a searcher is looking for a specific page, brand, or thing) may have a high pursuit volume, yet sitting for that term isn't most likely going to return many snaps.

This is a general headway of your expression framework, as it goes past trying to rank for high volume search terms, fairly focusing on the pursuits that will return the most snaps and warm prompts your business.

All around, navigational request terms are not worth your time.

Informational request terms (when a searcher is looking for additional information regarding a matter) give the best entryway to you to make a better piece of force content.

Getting a handle on inactive semantic requesting (LSI)

Inactive Semantic Requesting (LSI) is a cycle Google uses to all the more promptly handle the middle subject of a page and its particular circumstance. This ensures that it can give precise results to match a searcher's inquiry.

For instance, LSI helps Google with understanding whether a site page zeroing in on the expression "mermaids" is a page about the unbelievable creature mermaids or a page about the 1990 spoof show Mermaids.

Clearly, it's all of the associated expressions, comparable words, and articulations you moreover use on your site page that will help them with sorting out the remarkable circumstance.

Honestly, when you search for something on Google, they will in like manner highlight any associated words and articulations in solid for every result.

You can use Google's LSI collaboration to track down exact related watchwords to overhaul your substance. This further diminishes expression stuffing, outfitting you with an abundance more Site streamlining appropriate articulations to focus on.

You ought to just enter your important expression into Google and scrutinize the striking words that appear in the bits of the results.

Expecting that you notice striking terms that can without a very remarkable stretch be associated with your own substance, you understand Google will believe your page to be a fair partner for that request.

Watchword Investigation Gadgets

You will require several Web architecture upgrade gadgets to use our general watchword research approaches.

We'll quickly run you through our proposition, including free expression assessment, orchestrating, and competitor examination contraptions.

Google Watchword Coordinator Image of Google Expression Coordinator

Need to rank #1 on Google?

Go right to the source and sort out search volumes and Google floats straightforwardly from the source.

This is a free gadget, but you ought to make a Google Advancements record to get to it.

The revelation choice is intended to assist you with finding new watchwords applicable to your site, business, and items.

Though the hunt volume choice will give you information for a rundown of watchwords you as of now have.

This instrument targets Adwords clients who need to run CPC promotions, so it offers information on Advertisement expenses and catchphrase offering.

Nonetheless, you can in any case utilize these apparatuses to find the right Website design enhancement catchphrases for you.

The HOTH FREE Watchword Organizer Apparatus

The HOTH Free Google Watchword Organizer Apparatus

This isn't simply an improper fitting, our catchphrase research instrument is an incredible option in contrast to setting up a Google Promotions record and mission.

Fuelled by SEMrush, this easy to use organizer instrument makes it simple for anybody to find high-volume terms connected with your center watchword.

It's essentially as straightforward as composing in your fundamental watchword and hitting "view catchphrase research."

Moz Catchphrase Adventurer

Moz's convenient instrument makes it truly simple to find an entire bundle of key terms connected with your objective question.

Each catchphrase research device will offer a rundown of terms that are connected with your particular watchword search.

Moz's instrument is unique since it goes that additional length to offer parallel terms that you won't see proposed elsewhere.

This is perfect for finding those high-changing over lengthy tail expressions and questions.

They likewise offer a "need score" for every catchphrase, consolidating search volume and trouble information to assist you with picking which explicit terms and expressions to target.

Ahrefs Watchword Generator

In the event that you're searching for a device that simplifies it to separate between the simple and hard watchwords to rank for, Ahrefs device utilizes a traffic signal framework that is really plain as day.

The free variant of the instrument likewise permits you to separate between question watchwords and customary catchphrases, which is perfect for creating Search engine optimization blog content thoughts.

Their superior exploration instrument is likewise one of the most clever out there, giving explicit data on the number of backlinks you should rank first page for a specific term.

The HOTH Watchword and Content Hole Investigation Instrument

Take your catchphrase procedure to a higher level and guarantee you are beating your rivals with this whole investigation device.

You can enter your space name and up to 3 contenders to analyze the catchphrases you are focusing on and positioning for.

This is perfect for offering a new knowledge to look through you could have missed or ought to be moving your concentration to.

Soovle

Assuming you're searching for catchphrases past driving web crawlers like Google and Bing, Soovle is your all inclusive resource for scratching watchwords from across the web.

Assuming your center is Online business or you have a multi-channel content promoting system, this is a shrewd method for learning about watchwords that might have gotten away from your rival's grasp.

SECockpit

SECockpit is an instrument that works very much like numerous other exploration devices on this rundown - you enter a catchphrase, and it uncovers an extensive rundown of ideas and their important experiences.

Notwithstanding, SECockpit's bits of knowledge take information from Google's Catchphrase Organizer and go more inside and out than some other instrument on this rundown.

Albeit the information will be valuable for novices, it will be Website design enhancement professionals who can really comprehend what it implies.

You can tap on any catchphrase to uncover contest measurements for the term's main 10 outcomes, including their backlink profiles and a breakdown of day to day traffic.

Email Promoting Computerization and Division

Email showcasing computerization is tied in with making limited time crusades a robotized cycle. How could it be helpful? Mechanizing messages saves advertisers the issue of making and sending new messages each time when a possibility shows interest in a brand, a client forsakes a truck, business dispatches a deal, etc. Beside that, studies have shown that using exhibiting mechanization programming prompts a 80 percent increment in the quantity of leads and a 77 percent support in changes.

The following are five motivations behind why each advertiser ought to carry out email showcasing computerization. One can:

- **Make portioned mailing records**

Email advertising mechanization empowers organizations to make exceptionally fragmented mailing records. Advertisers can portion their rundowns in view of endorser exercises and Client Relationship The executives information (whole buy history, last buy, lead stage, and so on.)

From viable sectioning, advertisers can harvest profoundly designated promoting robotization work processes that augment the two deals and commitment.

- Convert possibilities into clients

Email is an ideal device for lead sustaining. Email robotization assists advertisers with sustaining the leads that they need to change over through their deals pipe really. It guarantees that they stay away from the escalated undertaking of sending showcasing messages physically.

- **Stay aware of responsibility with potential outcomes and existing clients**

Email advertising mechanization furnishes online advertisers with navigational information that empowers them to recognize which resources or connections inside their messages get ideal reactions. By considering this data, advertisers can then improve the adequacy of the messages in their messages to keep away from protests, fabricate positive brand impressions, and decrease the quantity of withdrawals and skips. In the end,marketers get to keep up with solid degrees of commitment with the two possibilities and clients.

- **Increment proficiency**

With email robotization, online advertisers can modernize redundant CRM undertakings and save a great deal of time and exertion. A portion of the exercises they can robotize include: putting away and following client information, deciding the degree of premium of their clients and their goal to purchase utilizing lead scoring, restoring contact with idle leads, working out profit from speculation (return for money invested).

Further develop commitment

Email robotization empowers advertisers to give proper, customized, and ideal messages to their supporters. Thus, advertisers help the commitment endorsers have with their image.

Email advertising mechanization enjoys a few benefits. These are:

- **Expanded exchanges**

Email computerization grants promoters to give tweaked fields, for instance, name, region, association name, and so on, in email messages.. Modifying showcasing messages in this manner brings about open rates expanded by 26%. Likewise, it is important that messages with customized messages lead to an exchange rate that is multiple times higher.

- **Successful division**

Email showcasing robotization assists advertisers with conveying pertinent messages to their endorsers. It permits brands to fragment (in view of information) the two leads and clients into various gatherings to guarantee that they get the offers they're keen on.

As per MailChimp's review, divided email crusades have 100.9 percent higher navigate rates and 14.3 percent higher open rates.

Expanded income with value-based messages

Value-based messages will be messages shipped off site guests consequently after they play out a particular activity, for instance, downloading a digital book, buying, etc. Email advertising computerization permits proactive advertisers to utilize conditional messages to go to different lengths. For instance, an email for certifying a solicitation could likewise consolidate "Relative

Things" at the lower part of the message.. With value-based messages alone, organizations can acquire up to multiple times more income.

 Incorporate with the client purchasing cycle

Email mechanization permits advertisers to adjust their business exercises with the buy pattern of their clients.It enables you to send messages right about the time a client needs a greater amount of their things. For example, on the off chance that a client buys fade one time each month, an advertiser can plan a special email that goes out to the client following a month.

Email robotization is about triggers and activities. Right when a particular event is set off, a specific email or set of messages are sent. The length of a mechanized email series relies upon the quantity of promoting activities the business needs to computerize. The advertiser can, thusly, be essentially as imaginative as they need in the sort of satisfaction they ship off endorsers. To empower email advertising computerization.

Utilizing work processes, organizations can send the ideal messages to leads with flawless timing in view of the data they have about them.

By following the exercises of leads when they are drawing in with the brand, advertisers can accumulate experiences and use them to set sets off that will send the most applicable messages. An email administration, for example, SendPulse assists with setting up and tweaking these triggers or occasions as per the advertiser's determinations.

Email advertising mechanization can be utilized for both B2B and B2C organizations. The two sorts of organizations can utilize computerization streams to send welcome messages, re-commitment messages, or criticism demand messages.

 B2B brand set triggers for the going with exercises:

A visitor sees a particular page on a business' site.

A chance starts following the business by means of online diversion.

A potential client shows repeated interest in unambiguous things or organizations introduced by the association anyway doesn't interface.

New or existing client changes over.

Organizations ought to exploit email showcasing robotization to arrive at imminent clients as well as to improve associations with existing clients.

How to computerize email showcasing in SendPulse?

SendPulse permits organizations to set up and screen work processes rapidly and advantageously. To begin, join in sendpulse

Stage 1: Go to the Computerization 360 tab

On the client dashboard, click on "Computerizations," then, at that point "Make new mechanization" and select Robotization 360. This device permits the advertiser to set up mechanized messages, SMS, and web move set off by specific occasions or conditions and ship off an endorser on a current mailing list.

Stage 2: Pick an occasion

Select a beginning occasion or condition. It may very well be a specific date, for example, a birthday, a contact webhook, or a custom occasion set by the client. At the point when this start occasion is set off, the robotization stream promptly starts. For an effective mission, set a trigger in view of the way of behaving of beneficiaries on the data set.

Stage 3: Make a mechanization stream

Start making the robotized stream beginning with the occasion set. There is a settings board where one can change particulars about the robotization stream. Use "conditions" to set the subsequent stage in the mechanization stream and "channel" to customize messages in light of orientation, area, etc. etc.etc.Computerization 360 likewise allows sponsors to manage their mailing records. One can copy, move, update, or delete contacts on a summary.

Stage 4: Screen transformations

Change is the achievement of the objective, as indicated by the advertiser. It tends to be open rate, clicks-thro. A request affirmation email is sent following a client makes a request. It gives the client fundamental insights concerning the buy to check.

Much thanks to you email

A thank you email is sent after a guest buys in or makes a buy. It is an essential way for a business to cultivate individual client connections.

Pay-Per-Snap Publicizing and Online Entertainment Remarketing

PPC represents pay-per-click. It's a sort of computerized showcasing where you pay each time a client taps on one of your promotions. To see what PPC promotions resemble, run practically any hunt on Google (or Bing). You'll see advertisements showed at the highest point of the outcomes page:

See the postings at the top stamped "Supported"? Those are PPC search promotions from Google Promotions, Google's promotion stage.

PPC is at times alluded to as CPC. Be that as it may, there's an unpretentious distinction.

Cost per click characterizes the real sum a sponsor paid per click. What's more, PPC is the term for pay-per-click promotion.

You can run PPC promotions in different spots, including:

Web search tools like Google and Bing

Web-based entertainment stages like Facebook and Instagram

Flags on sites

Recordings on YouTube

Commercial centers like Amazon

Why Is PPC Significant?

PPC advertising can assist with drawing in new clients and develop your business. By making your image apparent to explicit crowds and taking them to high-esteem pages that help your business objectives.

How about we investigate what makes PPC so important:

- PPC Advertisements Take into consideration Successful Focusing on

PPC advertisements permit you to contact profoundly unambiguous crowds, in light of quite certain rules known as focusing on. So you address the ideal individuals and try not to squander promotion spend. The specific focusing on choices differ contingent upon the stage. Google Search has different focusing on choices contrasted with Facebook.

You could target clients who previously visited your site or drew in with your image. This is known as remarketing, or retargeting. This empowers you to help the possible client to remember your contributions. What's more, urge them to return and change over

- PPC Advertisements Drive Quick Outcomes

With PPC, you can begin driving traffic exactly the same day you start your mission. This is much faster than website improvement (Web optimization).

Website design enhancement can require a very long time to begin driving outcomes.

- PPC Advertisements Are Financially savvy

With PPC, you have command over your spending plan.

You conclude ahead of time the amount you need to spend altogether, and per click. Also, you possibly really pay when somebody taps on your promotion.

This, combined with strong focusing, implies you have a decent possibility of contacting a pertinent crowd at a cost that appears reasonable for you (we'll address this more when we examine the offering).

- PPC Is Not difficult to Gauge and Track

PPC promoting gives considerably more information and investigation than conventional types of advertising. In this way, it's straightforward the way in which your promotions are performing.

You'll presumably never know the number of individuals that saw your board or read your magazine promotion. Be that as it may, you can undoubtedly follow the number of individuals that tapped on your PPC promotion and what they did from that point. Like make a buy.

You can check whenever the number of snaps and transformations your advertisements that have produced in whichever stage you're utilizing:

- It's Not difficult to Oversee and Make Changes

At the point when you deal with a PPC crusade, you can undoubtedly set and change the greatest expense per-click, distribute spending plans, and change your procedure on the fly.

This degree of control empowers you to streamline your mission and adjust rapidly if necessary. Like supporting the financial plan of advertisements that are getting along nicely. Furthermore, stopping or making changes to promotions that aren't performing.

- It Assists You With acquiring (Free) Brand Mindfulness

Indeed, PPC produces snaps and transformations. But on the other hand it's really great for brand perceivability.

In any event, when clients don't tap on your advertisements, they actually see your image and message. Also, best of all, you possibly pay assuming that they click.

Thus, a lot of individuals could have eyeballs on your image. What's more, you won't pay a penny in the event that they don't click.

It Dovetails with Website optimization

Pay-per-click advertising and Website optimization complete one another. By running Website optimization and PPC simultaneously, you can consume more screen space in web search tool results. Which is probably going to drive more traffic and deals by and large.

Website optimization centers around neglected search rankings. Also, PPC supplements it by giving practically quick perceivability.

PPC versus Search engine optimization

Search engine optimization and PPC are both computerized advertising channels organizations can use to drive traffic.

Web optimization is centered around assisting your site with positioning higher in natural web crawler results. Also, driving more traffic.

Be that as it may, PPC incorporates paid search and different channels like paid social and show.

The principal distinction is this:

PPC includes paying per click

Web optimization (natural pursuit) clicks are free

By and large, organizations see the best outcomes when they adjust Web optimization and PPC in their promoting procedures.

You can begin to drive traffic with PPC from web search tools rapidly. However, it for the most part requires investment to naturally rank.

Search engine optimization and PPC can, and ought to, cooperate to drive achievement on the web.

How Does PPC Promoting Function?

Pay-per-click publicizing utilizes a straightforward interaction:

-Pursue a promoting account with Google Advertisements or the stage you need to run advertisements on

-Conclude who you need to target in light of catchphrases and different rules like socioeconomics

-Set your general spending plan and the amount you're willing to pay for each snap

-Make the duplicate and pictures/recordings for your promotions

-Send your promotion into a closeout with different publicists who are offering on similar watchwords or focusing on standards

-Trust that the bartering will decide whose advertisements will be shown — and where

-Pay when someone clicks your promotion

There are a wide range of stages and promotion designs (inclining further toward those later). And, surprisingly, various procedures. Be that as it may, the fundamental standards remain.

How the Google Promotions Advertisement Closeout Functions

At the point when a client plays out an inquiry, a promotion closeout happens. Google utilizes Promotion Rank to choose which advertisements to show, and in which request. Promotion Rank comprises of different elements, including:

Bid sum (the sum you're willing to pay)

Closeout time promotion quality (counting anticipated active visitor clicking percentage, promotion significance, and point of arrival experience)

Promotion Rank edges (the base value expected to show your advertisement)

Seriousness of a sale

Setting of the individual's inquiry (like area, gadget, season of search, the idea of the pursuit terms, different advertisements and query items showed on the page, and client signals)

Expected effect of resources and other promotion designs

One more significant idea to comprehend is Quality Score (QS).

Quality Score (QS) is a score somewhere in the range of 1 and 10 that Google gives every one of your promotions. It comprises of:

The normal active visitor clicking percentage (CTR) for a promotion — the number of individuals it that appraisals will tap on the advertisement contrasted with how frequently it's shown

The promotion's pertinence to the inquiry being looked

The point of arrival experience for the page that the promotion coordinates to

While Quality Score itself is not generally utilized in the Google Promotions advertisement sell off, these three parts are. So you'll need to watch out for your Quality Score to guarantee you're getting ideal promotion situations and estimating.

To actually take a look at your Quality Score, open Google Promotions, explore to "Crowds, watchwords, and content," then, at that point, click "Search catchphrases." This will raise an outline of catchphrase execution.

Key Parts of Google PPC Promotions

Presently, we should investigate the nuts and bolts of search promotion crusades.

Crusade Financial plan

You can set your main goal's ordinary everyday monetary arrangement considering what you want to spend. Remember that Google Promotions can spend up to twice your day to day financial plan on a specific day. Yet, Google won't charge more than your month to month financial plan.

Google utilizes 30.4 days out of each month. You can utilize this to compute your typical day to day financial plan in view of your month to month budget:So, set your day to day spending plan to $16.45 if you would rather not spend more than $500 in a month.

Cost

The expense of your PPC advertisements fluctuates in view of how cutthroat the sale is. What's more, how well your promotions perform.

In any case, you have some control over the amount you spend. You indicate the greatest CPC. Which is the most noteworthy sum you're willing to pay for each snap on your promotions. What's more, since it's a sale, you probably won't pay everything for each snap. You just have enough compensation to clear the Promotion Rank edge (least cost for your promotion to be shown) and beat any contenders underneath you. Along these lines, you could pay considerably less than your most extreme CPC.

Crusade Construction

Your PPC account is separated into crusades, promotion gatherings, and watchwords.

- **Crusades**

Each mission contains numerous promotion gatherings. You'll likely just have a few missions in your record (except if you're an enormous worldwide brand). On many occasions, missions ought to be founded on put forth objectives, focusing on, sort of promotions, or how you need to distribute spending plans. For instance, suppose you're running promotions for a vehicle sales center. You could set up various lobbies for "utilized vehicles" and "new vehicles" to keep spending plans, focusing on, and different changes isolated.

- **Promotion Gatherings**

Promotion bunches contain different related advertisements.You can consider them explicit gatherings of promotions that are set off by watchwords.Furthermore, you can incorporate various catchphrases (and match types) inside a promotion bunch.

Catchphrases

Catchphrases are words and expressions you pick that mean quite a bit to your business. At the point when a client looks for that watchword, your promotion can be shown.

At the point when you add a catchphrase to your record, you should choose a watchword match type. Match types permit you to control which search terms will set off your advertisements.

Watchword Match Types

The Google watchword match types you can utilize are:

Expansive match: Promotions might show on look through connected with your watchword — giving you minimal measure of command over what sets off an advertisement yet the most stretched out reach. This incorporates incorrect spellings, equivalents, related look, and other related varieties. For instance, utilizing the catchphrase "get-away Hawaii" could likewise make your promotions appear for "excursion arranging Hawaii" and "lodgings Honolulu." Yet not for watchwords with totally various implications like "positions in Hawaii."

State match: Promotions might show on look through that incorporate the significance or inferred importance of your catchphrase. State match offers more extensive reach than careful match (we'll get to that in a second), however it's somewhat more unambiguous than wide match. For instance, focusing on the watchword "get-away Hawaii" would likewise have your promotions appear for "occasion Hawaii," "excursion Hawaii thoughts," and "summer outing to Hawaii."

Definite match: Promotions might show just on look with the specific importance or plan of your catchphrase. This gives you the most impenetrable command over the terms that trigger a promotion however minimal measure of reach. A quest for "get-away Hawaii" could set off a promotion for "excursions in Hawaii."

Negative watchwords: Advertisements won't show in looks for catchphrases you need to bar. This is a compelling method for forestalling squandered spending plan and superfluous traffic.

Offering Techniques

Google offers various offering techniques. You can pick which technique is best for you in light of whether you need to zero in on getting clicks, impressions, transformations, or perspectives. If you have any desire to zero in on changes, Google offers five kinds of Savvy Offering techniques. These are robotized offered procedures that utilization Google's computer based intelligence to advance for changes or transformation esteem:

Target cost per activity (CPA): This offering system assists you with controlling the amount you need to spend on each ideal activity, similar to a buy or a sign-upTarget return on promotion spend (ROAS): This offering technique allows you to lay out an objective for how much cash you need to make as a trade-off for each dollar you spend on promotions, assisting you with boosting benefit

Boost transformations: This offering technique includes the stage consequently changing your offers to get whatever number individuals as could reasonably be expected to make a particular move on your site, like making a purchase or wrapping up a design

Expand transformation esteem: This offering procedure helps you get the most worth out of your promotion financial plan via naturally streamlining your offers to drive higher-esteem changes, like bigger guys

Upgraded cost per click (ECPC): This offering methodology consequently changes your manual offers in light of the probability of a tick prompting a deal or other significant activity. In the event that you want to produce snaps to your site, you could attempt these bid methodologies:

Amplify clicks: This computerized offering procedure has you set a normal everyday financial plan, and Google Promotions will attempt to drive the absolute most snaps affordable.

Manual CPC offering: This offering system allows you to deal with your greatest CPC offers yourself. To give you greater adaptability. For instance, you can decide to set higher offers for top-performing promotion gatherings or watchwords. If you have any desire to zero in on brand mindfulness, you can attempt a bid procedure intended to boost perceivability. Like CPM (cost-per-mille or cost per thousand impressions).What's more, in the event that you're running a video crusade (on YouTube or the Google Show Organization), you can likewise pick CPV (cost-per-view) offering. It may very well merit evaluating at least one or two offering methodologies to see which turns out best for you.

Note: These methodologies are for Google Advertisements. Other PPC stages have comparative, yet unique, offering choices.

Best Compensation Per-Snap Stages

There are numerous PPC stages out there.

Here are the absolute most notable ones:

Google Advertisements

Google Promotions is the biggest PPC stage, with a portion of the overall industry of 28%.

Google Advertisements is comprised of two key parts:

Google Search Organization: Search advertisements on Google search, Google Guides, Google Shopping and search accomplices on non-Google sites.

Google Show Organization: Show promotions and recordings on YouTube, Gmail, Blogger, and 3 million accomplice sites and applications.

Meta Advertisements

Meta possesses two of the biggest online entertainment stages: Facebook and Instagram.You can utilize Facebook Advertisements Supervisor to run PPC promotions on both Facebook and Instagram.

Meta offers quite certain focusing on choices in light of socioeconomics and interests. This, joined with colossal reach, empowers brands to take advantage of a gigantic pool of possible clients.

TikTok Advertisements

TikTok is a well known short-structure video stage. What's more, TikTok Promotions can be an incredible method for contacting a more youthful and exceptionally drew in crowd. TikTok Promotions offers a scope of publicizing choices, incorporating marked hashtags and in-feed promotions. With 1.7 billion clients around the world, the stage is developing quickly and extremely famous with Gen Z.

Microsoft Advertisements

Microsoft Promotions offers a method for expanding your range past Google. You can target clients on Bing and accomplice destinations. The Microsoft Search Organization abilities 38.1% of U.S. work area look and 6.4 billion month to month look around the world. Furthermore, Microsoft claims that Microsoft Advertisements can associate you with 46 million searchers in the U.S. that Google can't reach.

LinkedIn Advertisements

With LinkedIn Advertisements, you can arrive at 900 million clients overall on the biggest virtual entertainment stage for proficient systems administration. LinkedIn Promotions offers progress focusing on choices, including position title, manager, industry, and expert abilities, making it ideal for B2B advertising.

Kinds of PPC Promotions

At the point when you run a PPC crusade, you have a wide choice of various promotion designs. The organizations accessible rely upon the stage.

Search Promotions

Search promotions show up on the outcomes pages of web search tools like Google when clients search for data.

Search advertisements are shown when clients look for significant catchphrases. This ensures your advertisements show explicitly to crowds looking for terms connected with your items or administrations.

For instance, a quest for "best doggy food" will raise supported results from pet food organizations.

Search advertisements give prompt perceivability and draw in your interest groups.

Show Promotions

Show promotions are standard or picture advertisements that show up on different sites inside the Google Show Organization and other accomplice locales. They can show up at the top, base, side, or elsewhere on a website page. They frequently appear on news destinations.

Video Promotions

Video promotions show up on locales across the web and video stages like YouTube. There are a wide range of kinds of video promotions. A typical one is a pre-roll promotion that is displayed before the video the client needs to watch.

The most effective method to Make a PPC Mission with Google Promotions

Here are the means you want to take to set up a PPC crusade. This is for Google Promotions, yet the means are comparative for other PPC stages.

Set Up a Record: To begin with, you really want to make a Google Promotions account. It's free. You'll simply have to enter your email address and pick a secret key.

Select Your Objective and Mission Type: The specific advances can change contingent upon various elements, similar to your area. Typically, you'll begin by picking an objective and mission type. This is the way you make it happen:

Open Google Promotions and snap "Make." Then, at that point, click "Mission.

As of now, you'll be approached to pick your goal. Google will suggest various channels in light of what your objectives are. For example, to drive "Brand mindfulness and reach" Google will suggest Show and Video.To browse every accessible channel, simply click "Make a mission without an objective's guidance."Next, select a mission type. There are a wide range of choices, including "Search," "Show," "Shopping," "Video," "Application," and that's just the beginning.

Suppose you need to run a mission on Google search. You would click "Search," then "Continue."Then, you can choose the outcomes you might want to get from your mission, for example, site visits. In any case, you don't need to. Google simply gives you some additional assistance during the arrangement interaction in the event that you do.

Lastly, name your mission and snap "Proceed."

Then, select what you need to zero in on. "Clicks" is a decent choice to begin with, particularly in the event that this is your most memorable mission.

Pick an Offering System and Put forth Your Line

You'll have to conclude the amount you need to spend per click. What's more, which offering procedure you need to utilize.

During the mission arrangement, you can really look at the container "Set a greatest expense for each snap bid breaking point." Or, you can leave it clear and set as far as possible at the promotion gathering or catchphrase level later.

At the point when that is no joke, "Next."

Not certain the amount you ought to be paying per click? Research the typical CPCs for your industry and change after some time in light of return for money invested (profit from speculation).Design Your Mission Settings and Focusing on

You want to pick where your promotions will be shown.

To show your promotions on Google search just, guarantee the containers "Incorporate Google search accomplices" and "Incorporate Google Show Organization" are not checked during effort setup:Then, look down and pick where you maintain that your mission should run.

Assuming that you're attempting to target clients who live in a specific nation, select that country.

Then, click "Area choices" and select "Presence: Individuals in or consistently in your designated areas." Of course, Google will show your advertisements to individuals who are likewise keen on the country. Be that as it may, this isn't generally a decent choice. Like for a French furniture brand that doesn't send globally.

Then, select the dialects your clients speak:If you click "More settings," you'll track down a couple of additional choices.

A few vital things here are the beginning and end dates.

Choose when you'd like your mission to begin and wrap up. In the event that it's a consistently on crusade, you can simply leave the end date as "not set."

Enter Your Catchphrases and Transfer Your Promotion Resources

Then, you'll come to a segment called "Watchwords and promotions." You'll need to name your promotion gathering to consider what you're centering. Click the pencil symbol close to "Promotion bunch 1." And change the name to something significant.

Then, enter the watchwords for that promotion bunch. Google offers you a couple of ways of tracking down catchphrases.

You can then enter the item page where it says "Enter a URL to filter for watchwords." Or, you can type catchphrase thoughts where it says "Enter items or administrations to promote."

It's ideal to explore your catchphrases and gathering them before you start the Google Advertisements arrangement. This gives you additional opportunity to track down the best catchphrases and settle on a design.

To find the best catchphrases for your mission, you can utilize Watchword Wizardry Device. Type in a seed catchphrase (a wide watchword connected with your business or item). Like "doggy food."

Also, click "Search."Select the watchwords you need to utilize, click the "+ Add to catchphrase list" button, and name your rundown. On the off chance that you have a ton of catchphrases, it's really smart to divide them into gatherings. These are called groups.

Click on the name of your rundown to open it. Then, at that point, click "Bunch this rundown." And the apparatus will divide your watchwords into groups for you: Then, at that point, reorder the catchphrase bunches into Google Advertisements.

A typical construction is to utilize one bunch for every promotion bunch. You may likewise need to part your promotion bunches in light of a typical subject, similar to items you offer.

Make Your Promotions

Then, look down to the "Advertisements" segment in Google Promotions. This is where you can make your advertisements, precisely as you maintain that they should be shown.

Where it says "Last URL," enter the URL of the page you need to direct people to.

Under "Show way," demonstrate how you maintain that the connection should be shown.

For instance, on the off chance that you maintain that the connection should be clothesbrand.com/pants you would enter "pants." On the off chance that you leave it clear, it will be equivalent to your space (clothesbrand.com).

Then, you really want to compose your promotions. Make a few infectious titles and up to four depictions so Google can show various variants and see which performs best.

Beware of as far as possible. You can really take a look at the review on the right-hand side to guarantee your promotions look how you expected.

At the point when that is no joke, "Next."

Set Your Spending plan

Presently, now is the right time to set your financial plan. Conclude the amount you might want to spend each day founded on the equation we examined before that isolates your month to month financial plan by 30.4.

Then, enter that number in the crate under "Set custom financial plan." And snap "Next."

Audit Your Mission

It's currently time to audit your mission.

Google Promotions will show you an outline of the settings you've picked and the advertisements you made.

On the right-hand side, Google will show you a Mission Streamlining Score. Which provides you with a thought of how all around enhanced your advertisements are.

Twofold actually look at everything, including your mission settings, watchwords, promotions, and financial plan.

Assuming everything is all together, click "Next." Google will survey your mission and push it live whenever it's endorsed. This can require a couple of moments or several hours.

CHAPTER 6: INFORMATION DRIVING NAVIGATION

Information driven direction (DDDM) is characterized as utilizing realities, measurements, and information to direct essential business choices that line up with your objectives, goals, and drives. At the point when associations understand the full worth of their information, that implies everybody — whether you're a business expert, project supervisor, or human asset trained professional — is engaged to settle on better choices with information, consistently. In any case, this isn't accomplished by just picking the suitable examination innovation to recognize the following key as an open door. Your association needs to pursue information driven choice making the standard — making a culture that supports decisive reasoning and interest. Individuals at each level have discussions that begin with information and they foster their information abilities through training and application. Fundamentally, this requires a self-administration model, where individuals can get to the information they need, offset with security and administration. It likewise requires capability, setting out preparing and improvement open doors for representatives to master information abilities. At last, having leader promotion and a local area that backings and settles on information driven choices will urge others to do likewise.

Laying out these center abilities will assist with empowering information driven independent direction across all occupation levels so business gatherings will consistently address and examine data to find strong experiences that drive activity.

Web Examination and Client Conduct Investigation

We are in the powerful domain of the present computerized scene. What's more, the significance of examination for a site we can't overemphasize. Sites have become basic stages for organizations to communicate with their crowds. Hence, understanding client conduct has become foremost. All things considered, this is the way you can make progress. Web investigation has arisen as a strong tool stash permitting site proprietors to acquire priceless experiences into the intricate dance among guests and their virtual climate.

Web investigation is, at its center, the logical act of assessing client communication. Web investigation innovations help to tackle the riddles of online commitment. Different high level apparatuses and advancements are accessible to you. Web examination devices track and gather data about site guests. They gain proficiency with an abundance of data about their inclinations and level of contribution.

This approach permits site proprietors to translate the subtleties of client conduct. You will actually want to comprehend what reverberates with your crowd. Furthermore, this will assist you with settling on informed choices on advancing the circumstance. This text is devoted to the multi-layered field of web investigation. We need to reveal insight into its approaches, advantages, and key job in progress.We ought to set out on a trip of learning!

What is Web Investigation?

Web investigation is a precise course of gathering, estimating, examining, and deciphering information. It assumes a key part in both computerized showcasing methodology and site executives. Site client conduct examination gives noteworthy information. You can pursue choices to advance execution and accomplish business objectives.

In computerized showcasing, web examination fills in as a compass. It guides advertisers toward viable systems and missions. Track key measurements, for example,

Site traffic

Change

Commitment rate

You will actually want to assess the adequacy of your endeavors and change your methodology. Along these lines, you can accomplish a more prominent reaction from your ideal interest group. This approach permits you to refine your showcasing procedures. You will actually want to designate assets and distinguish learning experiences.

In site the board, the significance of site examination will permit you to acquire a complete perspective on client communications and comprehend how guests explore, cooperate with, and draw in with your site and content. The information gathered covers a large number of perspectives, including:

Traffic sources (reference destinations, web crawlers, direct visits

Client socioeconomics (geographic area, gadget type, program)

Their way of behaving (site hits, number of snaps, time spent on pages)

Concentrating on this information allows you to distinguish examples, inclinations, and trouble spots. It permits you to pursue vital choices. For instance, you comprehend which pages produce the most commitment. Or then again you comprehend where clients are probably going to quitter. It permits you to further develop your site construction and spot the right satisfaction. Basically, web investigation goes about as a route instrument. It guides you to examination and upgrades for UX and execution.

Key Measurements to Screen

Checking key examination measurements for a site is fundamental. It will provide you with a total image of client conduct and site improvement. The absolute most significant measurements to screen include:

Online visits. Online visits show what content reverberates with clients. Countless site visits shows that the substance is well known. Be that as it may, a low number of perspectives might demonstrate regions for development.

Skip rate. Skip rate estimates the rate that leaves a site subsequent to survey a solitary page. A high bob rate might demonstrate insignificant substance or low quality of administration.

Time nearby. This measurement uncovers how long clients spend on your site. Longer times frequently demonstrate connectedness with clients and convincing substance.

Transformation rate. The transformation rate tracks the level of guests who complete an ideal activity. It features the adequacy of invitations to take action and by and large client experience.

Active clicking factor (CTR). CTR estimates the adequacy of connections and invitations to take action. It helps on- site clients conduct examinations.

Client socioeconomics. Knowing client areas, dialects, and other segment information empowers designated content creation.

Search questions. Investigating search questions can uncover client goal and guide content creation. Every measurement gives novel bits of knowledge into client conduct. It allows you to go with informed choices to work on satisfaction, plan, and generally experience. By routinely observing and examining these measurements, you can create a guide.

Dissecting Client Excursion

Examination for UX fills in as a strong focal point. Through it, your emphasis will be on the mind boggling client venture. From the second a client enters the site to the finish of a transformation. Utilizing the information, site proprietors can outline and get a handle on the whole grouping of client corporations. Valuing the meaning of assorted touchpoints inside the client venture is fundamental. It permits you to uncover the substance of client conduct. You can distinguish which pages stand out, where commitment happens, etc. This all encompassing insight permits the organization to improve each touchpoint. You will actually want to give the accompanying:

Simple route

Customized content conveyance

Convincing invitations to take action

At last, concentrating on the client venture adds to figuring out the client's requirements. You'll have the option to investigate inclinations and problem areas. Furnished with this information, site proprietors can tweak and work on their contributions. You'll have the option to convey a more natural and charming excursion. It increments change rates as well as constructs continuous client dedication.Recognizing Trouble spots

Web examination apparatuses can assist you with perpetually distinguishing "trouble spots" in your webpage's exhibition. You might disapprove of the accompanying:

Ease of use

High bob rate

Also, different issues

You can recognize these issues via cautiously dissecting client ways of behaving. For instance, examinations show a high skip rate on a specific presentation page. It could show that the substance isn't meeting guest assumptions. Or on the other hand, for instance, your page has a sluggish stacking speed. By distinguishing these trouble spots, an organization can make a designated move. Along these lines, you can alleviate the issue and keep clients locked in.

Content Improvement

The significance of site examination will likewise help in happy streamlining. It will permit organizations to make and work on their web-based contributions. You will actually want to investigate measurements, for example,

Content ubiquity

Client commitment

Number of connection clicks

Along these lines, organizations can calibrate their substance systems. You will actually want to do this as per the crowd's inclinations. It will permit you to boost your effect. With examination information, organizations can figure out what sorts of content resound. It may very well be blog entries, recordings, infographics, or intuitive components. This information permits you to guide assets to make them more satisfied. You'll make content that clients find important through investigation for UX.

Client commitment measurements give understanding into the adequacy of content. Investigating this information uncovers what content is holding clients' consideration. Then you can reproduce fruitful commitment strategies in ongoing undertakings. Navigate rates give knowledge into the adequacy of invitations to take action. Research which CTRs are the best. It will permit you to refine your CTAs and further develop the client experience. Along these lines, examination information for a site permits you to improve content. You will transform client conduct into significant bits of knowledge. It permits organizations to make content that resounds. It connects with clients and guides them toward wanted activities. It makes a seriously captivating internet based insight and substantial outcomes.

Change Rate Enhancement (CRO)

Web examination assumes a key part in expanding change rates. It is all on account of transformation rate streamlining (CRO). CRO utilizes the information gathered to refine components of the site methodically. It eventually prompts an expansion in change rates.

The foundation of CRO is A/B testing. In it, you look at two forms of a page or component. It permits you to figure out which one gives a higher transformation rate. The quantitative premise of A/B testing is site client conduct investigation. It will permit you to go with informed choices in light of genuine client collaboration.

Pipe drop investigation includes examining the client's excursion from transformation section. What's more, you additionally distinguish the stages at which the client stops the interaction. Distinguishing trouble spots permits you to eliminate hindrances decisively. You can advance cycles and lessen skip rates.

Web investigation additionally directs the enhancement of Source of inspiration (CTA) components. Navigate, commitment, and transformation information assist with refining the plan and phrasing of CTAs.

Basically, web examination instruments permit organizations to come up with information driven techniques. They further develop client experience and eliminate hindrances. What's more, they improve the probability of changes. Through A/B testing, channel examination, and CTA streamlining, CROs influence the force of web investigation to increment changes and accomplish genuine business objectives.

Picking the Right Web Examination Devices

Picking the right web examination devices is a basic choice. It can altogether affect the outcome of your web-based business. Among the most famous choices are Google Examination and Adobe Investigation. They offer thorough data about client conduct and site execution.

While picking a web investigation device, you really want to think about a few elements. First and foremost, adjusting the device's abilities to explicit business objectives is central. For instance, for online business destinations, following transformation pipes and income is really important. For content destinations, commitment and client connection measurements are significant.

Adaptability is another key component. You ought to pick apparatuses that can meet your developing and evolving needs.

The apparatus' UI and usability are significant for powerful investigation. Openness to applicable measurements and customization choices can smooth out navigation and experiences extraction.

For better examination for a site, use instruments that incorporate with different devices. It will permit you to make an all encompassing information biological system and get further experiences.

Normally, you want to think about the expense too. Coordinate the speculation with the normal worth you get from utilizing the device.

While picking a web investigation instrument, be directed by the business' remarkable requirements. Like that, you'll guarantee it's good for reason to pursue informed choices and improve your internet based insight.

Setting Up Following

In this way, you definitely understand what web examination is. Presently we should figure out the customization. It includes a few vital stages. They will guarantee that the information is gathered and broken down precisely. Underneath we have given a bit by bit guide:

Choosing a web investigation instrument. Pick the right device, like Google Examination or another, in view of your requirements.

Make a record. Register a record on your preferred foundation and make another property for your site.

Create the following code. Get the following code or tag from the examination device. In Google Examination, this is a JavaScript piece.

Embed following code. Glue the following code into the header or footer of your site's HTML code. This code tracks client collaborations and sends information to the examination instrument.

Put forth objectives. Characterize explicit objectives (e.g., buys, recruits) you need to track and set them up in your examination account.

Occasion following. Carry out occasion following for client activities like snaps, downloads, or video sees. Append occasion labels to important components.

Web based business following. Set up a web based business following to screen exchange information, item execution, and income.

UTM boundaries. For examination for UX, use UTM boundaries in URLs. It will permit you to follow crusade sources, dissemination media, and different boundaries.

Testing and approval. Test the rightness of your following code utilizing various apparatuses.

Observing and examination. After customization, screen investigation reports consistently. You can get experiences in client conduct, commitment, and changes. Well known following codes and labels include:

- Google Investigation. General Examination or Worldwide Site Tag (gtag.js)
- Adobe Investigation. JavaScript following code
- Facebook Pixel. JavaScript code for following client associations and changes

LinkedIn Knowledge Tag. JavaScript code for following changes and site visits from LinkedIn promotions, Appropriately setting up following guarantees that you gather exact and important information. It will help you in upgrading your site and promoting endeavors.

Information Protection and Security

Guaranteeing consistency with information protection guidelines is vital while using web investigation. A few guidelines, like GDPR (General Information Security Guideline) and CCPA (California Buyer Protection Act), require straightforward assortment and handling of client information with client assent and quit. It includes:

- Giving an unmistakable protection strategy
- Getting express assent for information assortment

Giving clients components to deal with their information

To keep up with client information security while using web examination, think about the accompanying tips:

Guarantee information transmission security. The significance of site examination incorporates carrying out secure conventions (HTTPS). You want this to scramble information transmissions between clients' programs and your site.

Standard reviews. Routinely review your information assortment and capacity processes. Along these lines, you can distinguish weaknesses and guarantee consistency.

Admittance to client information. Limit admittance to client information to approved workforce as it were. Execute solid validation controls.

Information maintenance strategies. Lay out clear information maintenance and erasure arrangements. Store them just for the expected period.

Outsider sellers. While utilizing outsider web examination devices, you ought to pick solid merchants. They ought to focus on information security and agree with administrative prerequisites.

Assent the executives. Execute vigorous assent of the executives instruments. They ought to permit clients to control their inclinations. They ought to have the option to quit following in the event that they wish.

Follow security guidelines and information assurance best practices. It will keep clients' trust. Furthermore, it will be an extraordinary chance for you to make a site client conduct an investigation.

Web examination is a fundamental compass in the present computerized scene. It exhibits how firms might better figure out client conduct. Examination for a site supports the improvement of a site's presentation. Web examination gives up a universe of potential outcomes by assessing details. It empowers organizations to decipher shopper inclinations and distinguish issue issues. Utilizing web investigation isn't a choice. It is a changing need. Organizations might go with instructed choices by utilizing the capability of these advances.

Organizations are urged to gain by the commitment of web examination in an information driven future. You won't simply get an upper hand by utilizing this information. You will foster a client focused methodology. It will push long haul development, significant association, and consistent improvement.

A/B Testing for Change Rate Enhancement

Building a site that produces sufficient traffic to create deals is no simple undertaking. What's more, on the off chance that you've been becoming your online business for a couple of months at this point, you've probably had the option to get a good measure of income for your business. Be that as it may, the work doesn't stop there. Whenever you've had some verification of an idea, now is the right time to expand your deals by doing A/B testing to expand your transformations. In this article, we'll share what A/B Testing is, the reason you ought to run them, our own special trial and error work process, a model we've run here at Sprocket, and substantially more..Along these lines, could we make a dive.

What is A/B Testing?

A/B testing, here and there called split testing, is a trial and error technique wherein you contrast another variety with a control. The control would be the ongoing design, variety, title, or anything you might want to see a lift on for changes. The new variety is something definitely not the same as the control. Divide tests are normally performed on titles in messages, buttons on your site, duplicate changes on a presentation page, variety plans, or formats of a web composition.

For instance, you might've heard that red is the best tone for inspire buttons. That hypothesis emerged from a split-test. And keeping in mind that it tends to be valid on certain sites, others could find different varieties convert better contingent upon the format. You simply need to test it and see with your own eyes as what works for one site probably won't work for your own. There's an excessive number of factors impacting everything.

stomach muscle testing

Why You Ought to Run A/B Tests

1. To Build Transformations

A/B tests straightforwardly affect changes. By picking things to part test things that influence changes, like your site design, duplicate, or source of inspiration buttons, you can augment transformations on your site. For instance, you could see that the phrasing on your source of inspiration button just proselytes at 0.04% and you need to run a trial to check whether it could lift higher with an alternate word set. You can attempt another source of inspiration and run an investigation to see which wins out. On the off chance that there's a lift, you'd utilize the new variety. You can then run another analysis contrasting one more duplicate with the new victor to keep attempting to lift the transformations on your page.

2. To All the more likely Grasp Clients

A couple of years prior, a well known investigation to run was whether adding a video to your greeting page could add more transformations. Taking into account how well known video content is nowadays, it's nothing unexpected that video content on points of arrival changes over better, particularly for recordings with great creation esteem. You can investigate such countless things, which will assist you with better comprehension of what clients truly need and need to feel OK with purchasing from your site. The more tests you run, the more you'll comprehend what assists clients with their purchasing choices, so you can offer to a more prominent pool of individuals.

3. To Go with Information Informed Choices

It's so normal for us to change duplicates, plans, and designs in view of our own inclination. Once in a while things simply look or sound better with our own touch. However, tragically, that pleasantly sounding duplicate necessarily changes over worse. A/B testing advises us that what makes a difference toward the day's end is the information: does it bring more deals? By split-testing, you'll pursue information informed choices to guarantee your business is really productive. By checking on examination devices, seeing business numbers, and seeing the consequences of your Stomach muscle test, you'll have a superior by and large comprehension of whether a change on your site influences your vitally key exhibition measurements (KPIs).

increment transformations

Trial and error Work process

Around here at Sprocket, we have our own trial and error work process that we use to run A/B tests. You can utilize this work process to assist you with running split tests proficiently.

1. Disclosure and Exploration

The main phase of your trial and error work process for A/B testing is to zero in on research. During this period, you'll gather experiences that you can use to test thoughts. You'll explore thoughts to decide whether something merits testing or not.

2. Arranging

In the wake of arranging your thoughts as a whole, you really want to choose what to focus on. In the event that a trial will influence your whole site, you'll simply have the option to run each examination in turn to guarantee the best outcomes. During this stage, you'll make a guide which will assist you with figuring out which A/B tests to begin with. You could likewise investigate which necessities or assets are required for each test prior to proceeding it.

3. Test Improvement

During this period of parted testing, you'll have to gather together the entirety of your partners. Contingent upon the size of your organization, there might be various individuals chipping away at these split tests with you. For instance, in many associations, the three gatherings that work on A/B tests test to be: plan, designing, and content. You'll audit the test with all partners during this interaction.

4. Test Setup

During this piece of A/B testing, the split test is live. This isn't an ideal opportunity to roll out a fast improvement to a region of a page as you would influence the examination. You'll need to impede individuals from making changes to the page during this time for the most dependable outcomes. Illuminate your group not to roll out any improvements to each page the investigation is running on with a firm time period.

5. Test Results and Detailing

In the last phase of A/B testing, you'll figure out which of the two choices is the champ. Assuming you find your control is the champ, extraordinary, it implies you don't have to roll out any improvements. Assuming the variety is the champ, you'll probably need to execute that choice to profit from the lift in transformations. You could likewise need to make a report where you keep your tests as a whole and results in a similar spot, so particularly that as colleagues go along with you'll have the option to give individuals admittance to the setting they need.

How Long Ought to A/B Tests Run

A/B tests ought to run for between one to about fourteen days. It assists with covering all week long, at least, so you have no anomalies. Be that as it may, few out of every odd week is something similar. For instance, the seven day stretch of the biggest shopping day of the year is commonly not a great opportunity to run an examination. Numerous internet business organizations run a power outage period during that week where no improvement changes are finished during their pinnacle season to forestall any potential deals misfortune. So I mean to run your examination, during a one to fourteen day time frame beyond any huge occasions like Christmas, Easter, Mother's Day, or even fourth of July, deals occasions, or some other irregularities.

Illustration of A/B Tests

At Sprocket, we've run endless A/B tests to all the more likely to grasp dropshippers and showcasing all in all. What we've realized could intrigue you as well!

In one trial, we needed to see a lift in changes on the Shopify Application Store. In this way, we carried out changes to our pictures to detail the net revenue acquired on premium items, feature custom solicitations utilizing your own image's logo, featured delivery times and rebates on yearly plans, and referenced our broad assortment of items. By and large, each picture featured a critical advantage of why individuals ought to utilize Sprocket. The outcome? We had the option to increment transformations from 35% each week to 40% each week.

Shopify Applications for Running A/B Tests

With endless Shopify Applications accessible in the Application Store, you can undoubtedly run A/B test utilizing applications that assist with improving on the cycle for you. Pick the Shopify Application with the elements you really want. Each application offers something else, so do your own expected level of effort while picking a device that will assist you with performing precise split tests.

1. Shogun

Utilizing Shogun's page manufacturer, you can do A/B testing on your Shopify store. You can distribute up to 500 pages, contingent upon your arrangement, each with a custom design. The simplified page developer considers most extreme customization. As, just normal, you'd need to see which designs really convert the best. The A/B testing highlight is accessible on Shogun's Action plan for $99/month. Additionally, with an investigation suite for sure, you'll have the option to gauge your examinations easily and with information. Assuming that you might want to figure out how to run A/B tests with Shogun, the group has made an instructional exercise only for this component that you can look at here.

Stomach muscle testing application

A/B testing can step up the changes on your site without expecting you to expand your site traffic. Everything revolves around attempting new things to assist with expanding transformations. Whether you're running a split test to pick the best item picture or to increment changes on your landing page, a fourteen day A/B test can assist you with accomplishing a higher transformation rate. Furthermore, whenever you've expanded it, you can add more traffic realizing that you're not losing a larger number of deals than you ought to. In the event that you're keen on getting familiar with split tests, go ahead and leave a remark.

Using Large Information and AI

Large Information and AI have turned into the purpose for the outcome of different enterprises. Both these advances are becoming well known step by step among all information researchers and experts. Enormous information is a term that is utilized to depict huge, difficult-to-make due, organized, and unstructured voluminous information. Though, AI is a subfield of Computerized reasoning that empowers machines to consequently gain and improve for a fact/past information. Both AI and huge information innovations are being utilized together by most organizations since it becomes hard for the organizations to make due, store, and cycle the gathered information proficiently; subsequently in such a case, AI helps them.

Prior to diving in deep with these two most famous innovations, i.e., Large Information and AI, we will examine a speedy prologue to huge information and AI. Further, we will talk about the connection between enormous information and AI. Thus, we should begin with the prologue to Enormous information and AI.

What is Large Information?

Assortment of organized as well as unstructured information.

Huge information is an extremely immense field for anybody who is hoping to make a lifelong in the IT ventures

Challenges in Large Information

Huge information has colossal development and assortment of organized as well as unstructured information. Practically all organizations are involving this innovation for maintaining their business and to store, interact, and concentrate esteem from a mass measure of information. Consequently, it is turning into a test for them to involve the gathered information in the most productive manner. There are a couple of difficulties while utilizing Enormous information are, which are as per the following:

Catching

Arranging

Putting away

Looking

Sharing

MovingVeracity (Precision)

Dissecting

Visualizations

5 V's in Enormous Information

Enormous information is characterized by 5v's, which alludes to the volume, Assortment, worth, speed, and veracity. How about we examine each term separately.

What is Enormous Information and AI

Volume (Enormous volume of information)

Information is the center of any innovation, and the immense volume of information stream in the framework makes it important to select a unique stockpiling framework. These days, information is coming from different sources, for example, online entertainment destinations, web based business stages, new locales, monetary exchanges, and so on, and putting away information in the most effective manner is becoming ordered. Despite the fact that, with the progression of time, stockpiling cost is slowly diminishing, accordingly allowing capacity of gathered information. The gravitas that the term large information possesses is a result of its volume.

Assortment (Various configurations of information from different sources)

Information can be organized as well as unstructured and comes from different sources. It tends to be sound, video, text, messages, exchanges, and some more. Because of different configurations of information, putting away, making due, and sorting out the information turns into a major test for associations.Despite the fact that putting away crude information is easy, changing over unstructured information into an organized configuration and making them open for business utilizes is essentially intricate for IT skill.

Speed (speed at which information is handled)

Delivering and information arranging is exceptionally important to control information streams. Further, the predominance of handling information with high precision and speed is likewise essential for putting away, making due, and coordinating information in a productive way. Brilliant sensors, savvy metering, and RFID labels make it important to manage enormous information deluge in practically continuous. Arranging, surveying, and putting away such storms of information in an opportune style become important for most associations.

By and large, Veracity alludes to the precision of informational indexes. In any case, with regards to Enormous information, it isn't simply restricted to the precision of large information yet in addition lets us know how dependable the information source is. Further, it likewise decides the dependability of information and how significant it is for investigation. In one line, we can say Veracity is characterized as the quality and consistency of information.

Esteem (Significant information)

Esteem in Large Information alludes to the significance or handiness of putting away information for your business. In enormous information, information is put away in organized as well as an unstructured configuration, yet no matter what its volume, generally, it isn't significant. Thus, we want to change over it into a valuable configuration for the business prerequisites of associations. For e.g., information having absent or ruined values, missing key organized components, and so on, are not helpful for organizations to give better client support, make advertising efforts, and so on. Subsequently, it prompts lessening the income and benefit in their organizations.

Wellsprings of information in Large Information

Huge information can be of different arrangements of information either in organized as well as unstructured structure, and comes from different various sources. The principal wellsprings of enormous information can be of the accompanying kinds

Online Entertainment

Information is gathered from different online entertainment stages like Facebook, Twitter, Instagram, Whatsapp, and so forth. Despite the fact that information gathered from these stages can be in any way similar to message, sound, video, etcThe greatest test is to store, oversee and sort out these information in an effective manner.

Online cloud stages:

There are different internet based cloud stages, for example, Amazon AWS, Google Cloud, IBM cloud, and so on, that are likewise utilized as a wellspring of large information for AI.

- Web of things:

The Web of Things (WOT) is a stage that offers cloud offices, including information stockpiling and handling through IoT. Lately, cloud-based ML models are getting well known. It begins with summoning input information from the client end and handling AI calculations utilizing a fake brain organization (ANN) over cloud servers and afterward getting back with the result to the client once more.

Online Pages:

These days, consistently, a great many pages are made and transferred over the web. These pages can be as text, pictures, recordings, and so on. Consequently, these site pages are likewise a wellspring of enormous information.

What is AI?

AI is one of the most critical subsets of Man-made consciousness in the software engineering field. It is alluded to as the investigation of robotized information handling or dynamic calculations that work on themselves naturally founded on experience or previous experience. It makes frameworks equipped for advancing naturally and improves for a fact without being unequivocally modified. The essential point of an AI model is to foster PC programs that can get to information and use it for the end goal of learning.

With the ascent in Enormous Information, AI has turned into a vital participant in taking care of issues in different regions, for example,

Picture acknowledgment

Discourse Acknowledgment

Medical services

Money and Banking industry

Computational Science

Energy creation

Robotization

Self-propelled vehicle

Normal Language Handling (NLP)

Individual virtual help

Showcasing and Exchanging

The training area, and so on.

Distinction between Enormous Information and AI

What is Enormous Information and AI

With the ascent of huge information, the utilization of AI has likewise expanded in all ventures. The following is the table to show the distinctions between AI and large information as follows:

Distinction Between AI and Large Information

1. AI is utilized to anticipate the information for what was to come in view of applied information and past experience. While Big Information is characterized as huge or voluminous information that is challenging to store and furthermore can't be taken care of physically with customary data set frameworks.

2. AI can be sorted basically as directed learning, unaided learning, semi-regulated learning, and support learning. While Big Information can be classified as organized, unstructured, and semi-organized information.

3. It assists with dissecting input datasets with the utilization of different algorithms. It helps in examining, putting away, making due, and sorting out a gigantic volume of unstructured informational collections.

4. It utilizes apparatuses like Numpy, Pandas, Scikit Learn, TensorFlow, Keras. While large information utilizes devices like Apache Hadoop, MongoDB.

5. In AI, machines or frameworks gain from preparing information and are utilized to anticipate future outcomes utilizing different algorithms. While Big information predominantly bargains in separating crude information and searches for an example that assists with areas of strength for building making capacity.

6. It works with restricted layered information; thus it is moderately simpler to perceive features.While large information, It works with high-layered information; consequently it shows intricacy in perceiving highlights.

7. An ideal AI model doesn't need human intervention. While large information, It requires human intercession since it mostly manages a gigantic measure of high-layered information.

8. It is valuable for giving better client support, item suggestions, individual virtual help, email spam sifting, computerization, discourse/text acknowledgment, etc.   While large information, It is additionally useful in regions as different as stock showcasing examination, medication and medical care, farming, betting, ecological security, and so on.

The extent of AI is to make robotized learning machines that work on nature of prescient examination, quicker navigation, mental examination, more vigorous, etc. The extent of enormous information is exceptionally immense as it won't be simply restricted to taking care of voluminous information; all things considered, it will be utilized for enhancing the information put away in an organized configuration for empowering simple examination.

Enormous information with AI

Enormous Information and AI the two innovations enjoy their own benefits and aren't viewed for ideas or totally unrelated. Albeit both are exceptionally significant exclusively, when joined, they give the chance to accomplish a few fantastic outcomes. While discussing 5 V's in huge amounts of information, AI models assist with managing them and anticipate exact outcomes. Also, while creating AI models, huge information assists with separating top notch information as well as further developed learning strategies through giving investigation groups.

There is no mystery that practically all associations, like Google, Amazon, IBM, Netflix, and so on, have previously found the force of enormous information investigation upgraded by AI.

AI is an exceptionally pivotal innovation, and with enormous information, it has become all the more impressive for information assortment, information examination, and information joining. All enormous associations use AI calculations for maintaining their business appropriately. We can apply AI calculations to each component of Huge information activity, including:

Information Marking and Division

Information Investigation

Situation Reenactment: In AI calculations, we really want different assortments of information for preparing a machine and foreseeing exact outcomes. Be that as it may, now and again it becomes challenging to deal with this bulk field information. In this way, it turns into a test to oversee and dissect Huge Information. Further, this unstructured information is pointless until it is well deciphered. In this way, to utilize data, there is a requirement for ability, calculations, and processing foundation.

AI empowers machines or frameworks to gain from previous experience and use information obtained from huge amounts of information, and foresee precise outcomes. Subsequently, this prompts creating further developed quality business activities and building better client relationships with the executives. Enormous Information helps AI by giving various information so machines can find out more or different examples or prepare information.

In such ways, organizations can achieve their fantasies and get the advantage of large information utilizing ML calculations. Nonetheless, for utilizing the blend of ML and large information, organizations need gifted information researchers

The most effective method to apply AI in Enormous information

AI gives productive and robotized apparatuses to information social events, examination, and joining. In a joint effort with distributed computing prevalence, AI ingests spryness into handling and coordinates a lot of information no matter what its source.

AI calculations can be applied to each component of Large Information activity, including:

- Information Division
- Information Examination
- Reproduction

This multitude of stages are coordinated to make the higher perspective out of Large Information with experiences, designs, which later get sorted and bundled into a reasonable organization.

In this article, we have talked about Large information and AI independently and the essential distinctions between the two advances. Additionally, we have perceived how AI and large information can be utilized together to learn AI models utilizing the excellence of information from the gigantic measure of unstructured as well as organized information. Further, we have likewise seen a few applications that utilize enormous information and AI and give astounding outcomes.

CHAPTER 7: BUILDING SOLID CLIENTS CONNECTION

Great brands have consistently major areas of strength constructed with their client bases to empower client maintenance, extend deals portfolios, rouse rehash business, and transform clients into fans and brand advocates.

Be that as it may, in an economy progressively overwhelmed by web based business, building significant client connections has gotten more enthusiastic. While most brands have seen the size of their crowd decisively increase because of internet shopping and advanced advertising, scaling the personalization expected for trust and straightforwardness is confounded.

Why building client connections is significant

Solid client connections charm crowds to your organization and keep them in your environment. With such a lot of rivalry just a tick away, it's difficult to exaggerate the significance of building a compatibility with possibilities, clients, and backers.

Further develop client dependability. At the point when crowds realize a brand is faithful to them — recalling birthday celebrations, answering rapidly to client support necessities, and that's only the tip of the iceberg — they return that dedication in various ways. They may reliably pick you over the opposition, and they're additionally bound to become brand advocates over the long haul.

Lessen client stir. It's more savvy to keep a current client than it is to source and change over another one. Solid client connections expand your general return for money invested by continuing to showcase costs down.

Increment client lifetime esteem (CLV). More noteworthy brand dependability implies extra and bigger deals. Clients will pay something else for extraordinary assistance and will keep on getting back to your image in the event that you can assemble trust.

Making Remarkable Client Encounters

Client experience (or CX) is the way a client communicates with and feels about your image. Any time a client has some sort of touchpoint with your image, it's additional to the assortment of encounters that makes up their impression of your image. Basically, enough sure corporations and they'll be glad to stay a reliable client; enough regrettable encounters and they might very well at no point in the future think about you.

The following are a portion of the kinds of encounters a client can have with a business:

1. A client ventures into a retail location and is welcomed by a cordial specialist proposing to assist them with tracking down an item.
2. A client follows a business via online entertainment, and preferences a post that shows them a new thing.
3. A client needs to pay for an item, yet remains in line for 15 minutes on the grounds that only one clerk is working while the others talk among themselves.
4. A client visits a business' site and can undoubtedly find out about the administrations the business offers.
5. A client calls a business' administration line yet is dealt with discourteously and doesn't get their inquiry settled.
6. A client gets back to a most loved business since they love the feeling and environment.

Encounters regularly are not impartial. Clients will feel either decidedly or adversely about a touchpoint, and that inclination and feeling can influence the amount they'll enjoy with you or how steadfast they'll be, today and into what's to come. Fortunately business pioneers have some control over what sorts of encounters their clients have. In any case, why is zeroing in on encounters so vital?

For what reason Do Client Encounters Matter?

Client experience can represent the moment of truth your business. It's not just about whether they get the items and administrations they're chasing; it's likewise about building up the worth your image brings and getting future customers.Here are only a couple of motivations behind why putting resources into client experience is significant.

Encounters matter as much as items and administrations: Clients put a high worth on their encounters, and 80% of clients say that "the experience an organization gives is essentially as significant as its items or administrations."

There's higher maintenance for fulfilled customers:Positive encounters make fulfilled clients, and 90% of clients who are profoundly happy with a brand say they are almost certain to get back to that brand to make more buys.

Encounters influence income: Brands who focus on offering extraordinary encounters to their clients will see the positive effect on the primary concern, as 84% of organizations who further developed their client encounters saw expanded income. Zeroing in on encounters makes organizations stronger: Organizations that give extraordinary encounters to their clients are more impervious to showcase changes and downturns, and see "a shallower slump, bounced back more quickly, and accomplished multiple times the all out investor returns over the long haul."

Clients will pay a premium for experience: On the off chance that you offer your clients extraordinary encounters, they're more able to pay something else for your items and administrations — as much as 18% more.

Negative encounters have an effect, as well: Brands hoping to draw in and hold clients need to zero in on getting the encounters they give right reliably, since it would just take one terrible experience for 32% of clients to quit communicating with a brand.

How could organizations get expanded income and higher degrees of consistency? By zeroing in on how encounters drive the client venture.

What Encounters Mean for the Client Excursion

The encounters that you make for your clients straightforwardly influence their client process, or the way they take from learning about your image to turning into a long lasting fan. You can utilize encounters to further improve and drive their excursion in the accompanying ways.

Mindfulness: The initial step on the client venture is acquiring consciousness of your items, administrations, and brand, like catching wind of the brand from companions, or perusing a positive survey. This implies that they find out about your image from the positive encounters ahave previously had.

Thought: When a client has had some touchpoints with your image, they ideally begin to have a sufficiently positive outlook on their encounters that they would think about buying from you. Notwithstanding, in the event that a client has a negative encounter — the site is too difficult to even consider exploring, they can't track down somebody in that frame of mind to respond to their inquiries — they're probably going to forsake their thought of your image by and large.

Buy: Enough sure encounters with a brand will build their certainty that you're the one they need to give their cash to and will make a buy.

Maintenance: After the primary buy, brands have the chance to keep giving positive encounters to their clients by reconnecting them in new ways that offer some benefit and increment their ability to purchase.

Faithfulness: The last objective is long haul client reliability and maintenance. At this stage, clients have an emphatically enough outlook on your image to be a fan and evangelist, however this can occur assuming you keep on giving good encounters that build up their good sentiments about you.

Four Moves toward Making Extraordinary Client Encounters

Business pioneers who need to make extraordinary encounters for their clients should ponder about doing as such. In the event that you're setting out after thinking up a client experience system or need to work on your ongoing methodology, here's where to begin.

1. Conceptualize Your Client Experience System

Begin creating or further developing your client encounters by first coming up with a procedure or vision for what you need to mean for the client venture. For instance, on the off chance that your site has a high skip rate or deserted truck rate, upgrade your site insight. Assuming that your in-store buys have dropped off, take a gander at ways of expanding people walking through by further developing client care, offering more in-store innovation, or smoothing out the checkout cycle.

As you plan your technique, ask yourself what encounters you could make that:

1)align with and further your image

2)serve your interest group or client base

3)make the client venture more productive and frictionless

4)create more comfort

5)provide more cordial and information administration

6) make paying for items no fuss

Make certain to remember for your system what achievement resembles for you, and how you'll approach estimating accomplishment after rollout. Make clear goals of what you need to achieve, similar to additional buys, higher dollar sum per buy, or additional time spent on the site. Then, at that point, distinguish Key Execution Markers, or KPIs, that you can follow so you can decide whether you hit your objectives.

At last, as you assess your general client experience approach, consider making a chief job like a Client Experience Official (CXO) who could lead the creation,implementation, conveyance, and estimation of your client encounters.

2. Execute Your New or Further developed Client Encounters

Now that you've decided the sorts of encounters that will serve your clients and increase the value of their excursion, execute them.

In the first place, begin little. If you have any desire to carry out expanded reality in your in-store areas, don't carry it out across all areas on the double, yet pilot it in one area to figure out how it will function and assuming that clients are responsive.

Instruct clients on new encounters also. On the off chance that you're carrying out new self-administration requesting screens, have partners welcome clients over to the screens and show them how to utilize it.

Remember to advance your new encounters across your showcasing channels with the goal that clients can become amped up for the experience before they attempt it.

At long last, have a framework set up for following information and client input around your new encounters with the goal that you can check their effect, and use Client Relationship Director (CRM) programming to follow client contact focuses.

3. Measure Those Encounters with Information: Presently, now is the right time to gauge what your encounters mean for your business by social event information from your KPIs and breaking down the outcomes. Maybe you redid your site for a superior client experience, and found that your neglected truck rate went down and buys went up — accomplishing one of your objectives. Or on the other hand, assuming your information shows no change after your site redo, you realize that you really want to explore what else should be changed to hit your objective.

There are various measurements you can use to follow the progress of the encounters you make for your clients, which can include:

NPS: The Net Advertiser Score (NPS) just poses one inquiry: "How probably would you be to prescribe this organization to a companion?" Positive experiences lead to merry clients who need to tell others, and associations can follow that through their NPS.

Client degree of consistency: This measurement tells you at what rate you're keeping clients, and who is proceeding to draw in with your image. A high degree of consistency implies that clients are proceeding to track down esteem in the items, administrations, and encounters you offer.

Client agitate rate: This measurement tells you at what rate you're losing clients. This can assist you with deciding how and where commitment is dropping off, and whether your encounters are making clients leave.

LTV: The client lifetime esteem (LTV or CLV) can let you know how much a client has bought throughout the span of their relationship with your business. On the off chance that LTV increments, you realize you have a devoted client able to keep buying with you.

Measurements intended for your encounters: At long last, track measurements that will be influenced by your encounters. For instance, assuming you carry out an in-store experience that directs people to your site, track site visits, skip rate, time on page, and day to day guests. Assuming your encounters spin around expanding the sum per buy, go to your POS information to follow those numbers.

4. Enhance Your Encounters: At long last, utilize the experiences accumulated from your information to illuminate your system proceeding. You can gather every one of the information

you like, yet assuming you never break down that information for bits of knowledge that can assist with further developing your client encounter system, then why? Audit your new drives and utilize the bits of information collected to either keep up what you're currently doing, change your approach, or return to the arranging stage.

Executing Client Relationship The board (CRM) Frameworks

Completing business programming should never be a bit of knowing the past, especially concerning your client relationship with the leaders (CRM) programming. CRM structures have progressed into complex focuses that upgrade your association. Regardless, how well you coordinate a CRM system with your ongoing work interaction and business programming suite will coordinate its suitability. The best execution practices focused on your spread out goals, using a committed gathering to lead the execution and offering ready potential entryways that help delegates with understanding how to use the item when it is dispatched.

The best strategy to complete a CRM system

A CRM stage is a general structure update, and the scale and detail of its execution ought to match its normal reach. These six key thoughts make sense of the normal endeavor and approaches associations can follow for a powerful CRM execution process.

1. Set reasonable, critical targets.

reasonable of an individual writing down with images incorporating them

You should have an unquestionable and direct vision for your CRM clearly associated with your most central business capacities. List your full scale targets, record your overall vision for the CRM's impact, and pinpoint which CRM features and instruments will help you with achieving them.

A commonplace stumble in looking throughout these systems is considering the stages to be decoration or extensions rather than compromises. CRM systems really add new cycles and value, yet those are benefits, not targets. They could attempt to involve themselves from the fundamental mission. Present yourself a couple of direct requests while contemplating whether CRM writing computer programs is fitting for your association: Will the new system coordinate how you continue with work? Might it at any point be said that you are endeavoring to streamline a cycle or change it endlessly out?

"Put the cycle into the development," Barton Goldenberg, head of ISM and maker of CRM Ceaselessly: Empowering Client Associations, told Business News Everyday. The thing is just an instrument that makes the story."

His splendid rule? "Process first, people second, development third."

2. Do all important examinations to find the right CRM plan.

As the speediest creating business programming, CRM offers a tremendous field of decisions. Your specific mission statement is the most obliging goal, but slashing down the best three CRMs to your last choice is certainly more problematic than decreasing an inquisitively enormous summary. There is no single permanently established reaction - this is definitely not a mathematical test - but a couple of reactions are considerably more right than others.

The fundamental components in your decision could consolidate assessing, the significance of the CRM's gadgets to your cycle, accommodation and open blends. Keep the basic execution clear while staying aware of cognizance of what future upgrades could include. A fundamental yet viable farewell is more useful in both the short and long stretch than an unreasonably forceful execution that reaches out past your certification.

3. Select a CRM bunch driven by office champions.

gathering of partners meeting in an office

Whenever you have chosen the CRM stage that most intently lines up with your organization vision, you can prepare the creation unit. This requires a particular group to finish everyday jobs and steer progress. The group ought to incorporate these individuals:

Project supervisor (pioneer)

Frameworks designer (establishment)

Information expert (information relocation)

QA engineer (testing)

Champions (agents)

Contingent upon the size of your business and CRM execution, you might require more than one individual filling every job.

Alex Haimann, accomplice and head of business improvement at Less Irritating CRM, prescribes a group of champions to vouch for the item and go about as delegates between upper administration and its everyday clients.

"On any occasion some depiction of that little, exploratory gathering ought to be a place to pause sales rep," he said.

Your heroes are all around respected heads of each group who will essentially utilize the CRM. Haimann thinks of them as perhaps of your best resource in advancing reception of the CRM among your full staff, some of whom might be hesitant to change their everyday propensities and cycles.

"It should be conveyed that the CRM is an instrument that will help all levels inside the association," Haimann said.

4. Conjecture the expenses and advantages.

Work with your different groups to conjecture the particular impacts this CRM will have on your business during the execution cycle, the underlying a half year after send off as your group adjusts and the accompanying a year once the CRM is a proper piece of their everyday use.

Probably the most helpful reports are money saving advantage examinations and execution timetables. Be careful that creation might plunge during different phases of the rollout. Assets will be centered around establishment while representatives learn new practices, and general costs can increment relying upon the preparation and counseling administrations you select.

These substantial numbers will give you more precise assumptions to assist you with adjusting your significant objectives and accomplish purchase in from your chief group. Measurements that show the amount you hope to further develop client maintenance and change rates will persuade even the most wary. Yet, don't excuse their criticism; they might get a secret detail. In any case, their hesitance could continue to the next staff when unavoidable trouble spots emerge during the educational experience.

5. Move and incorporate information.

Cleaning your information and moving it into the new CRM stage will be the longest component of the execution. Indeed, even an ideal informational collection of your clients, funds and informing administrations that contains completely right and current data requires half a month to move. Absent or inaccurate information should be procured and fixed, or it will decrease the viability of your CRM.

Goldenberg says to initially conclude which information is important to move for you to limit the expenses and season of working with immaterial data. He has found that an excess of information, particularly at send off, turns into a weight on its clients.

6. Train the group and test the framework.

realistic of a director preparing a group of individuals before a larger than usual PC screen

When the CRM stage is functional, trust your bosses to lead preparing drives with their general staff. By this point, the heroes ought to know about the framework, its advantages and how to utilize the instruments.

Most CRM contributions incorporate preparation and counseling projects to empower organizations to capitalize on their foundation. During this testing stage, appoint your IT group to perform quality confirmation tests. A few bugs are unavoidable, however you don't maintain that the initial send off should be defaced by numerous dire IT fixes while the framework is live.

Significance of CRM execution

Another CRM framework will update many laid out processes for your group, so your arrangement should normally incorporate this new framework with your ongoing work process to plan representatives for its send off. A legitimate execution process limits the time required for representatives to become OK with its devices and furthermore mitigates risk.

An ill-equipped group will be less useful as they shuffle learning the framework with finishing their everyday jobs. Intensifying missteps while representatives utilize the product, for example, losing information or miscommunicating with their group, could hurt your income and client relations.

The more sections of your business the CRM contacts, the greater an execution system you require. Almost 50% of CRM executions neglect to live up to assumptions, and introducing a CRM framework without a definite procedure can prompt disarray, tainted information, despondent staff and injured efficiency as representatives work in reverse to figure out a new framework

Your group might utilize the CRM framework mistakenly without the essential preparation and asset speculation to get familiar with its highlights and practices, which restricts the worth of the whole buy, while possibly not by and large harming your primary concern.

How long does CRM implementation take?

The course of events for the execution of another CRM framework relies upon the size of the business and its different divisions. Nonetheless, most independent ventures can anticipate that execution should last one to 90 days. Other key factors incorporate which CRM arrangement you pick, whether you recruit outside help with information movement and framework testing, any preparation or counseling programs the CRM supplier offers, and the quality and amount of information you at present have.

Oppose the compulsion to simultaneously endeavor the various undertakings. CRM can carry far reaching developments to even the most essential cycles of your business, and missing any means could disrupt the whole interaction. Map out precisely when and how the means and preparing ought to happen to raise a ruckus around town running at send off.

Normal CRM execution slip-ups to keep away from

Doing an excess of too early

Overcomplication can change the focal point of a CRM with the goal that it settles some unacceptable issue. Haimann proposes a tight extension. "Put serious compliments on your best three or top five basic requirements."

Try not to endeavor to accomplish the essential objective of each and every division or client. There will constantly be valuable chances to overhaul your framework later on assuming that you start the correct way. Taking a different path is a lot harder in the wake of losing time, assets and possibly your group's trust after a troublesome send off.

Losing group support

Despite the fact that you see the master plan, you are likely less associated with the framework's everyday use than your group is. Pay attention to criticism and feel a debt of gratitude. Identify with representatives hesitant to change rehearses they might have utilized for a really long time.

Goldenberg stresses a "3X component" to show day to day clients the viability of a CRM. Whenever a client inputs a piece of information, "that client should get three significant snippets of data back to be roused to utilize the framework." A client who reliably sees the upsides of utilizing the product will perceive its handiness.

Failing to remember the motivation behind a CRM

A CRM stage is a device to assist your group with taking care of issues; it can't tackle the actual issues. Recall that the motivation behind a CRM is to enable the group, not for the group to engage the product. Adherence to that brilliant rule will keep your choices during the cycle zeroed in on the legitimate targets.

Stay away from normal mix-ups, for example, overcomplicating a send off process and failing to remember that the objective of CRM is to work as an answer for the group, not for the group to drive the CRM.

The best CRM programming

A solid execution might be significant, yet achievement begins with picking the right CRM programming in any case. To assist you with settling on the ideal choice for your business, we've sifted through many of the main arrangements available today to think of our rundown of the best CRM programming for independent ventures. Here is a gander at only a portion of the ones we picked:

Salesforce: An easily recognized name in CRM programming, Salesforce has long set the business standard and stays a go-to choice for some organizations. In our Salesforce survey, we viewed it as an exceptionally valuable, all-around item that could finish the work for private ventures.

Pipedrive: On the off chance that you love visuals, you'll adore Pipedrive. This CRM programming permits you to effectively construct visual deals pipelines with a simplified device that is natural and easy to use. During our Pipedrive survey, we viewed this as the greatest champion component the stage brought to the table.

monday: Assuming you're searching for CRM programming that ties into your task the board activities, look no farther than Monday. In our survey of monday deals CRM, we felt like the product organization's task the board roots radiated through. Interfacing your client to your inside cycles can yield strong outcomes, and monday is an extraordinary device to do precisely that.

HubSpot: As of now have a flourishing business programming suite and maintain that your CRM programming should plug into it flawlessly? In our HubSpot survey, we viewed the stage's many combinations as convincing. HubSpot can interface with practically any business programming you're now utilizing, assisting you with effectively sharing information across groups and offices.

Think about these close by our other best picks for a portion of the top CRM frameworks and the most helpful elements accessible at this point.

Arrangement for progress with your CRM programming

Executing a CRM programming so it suits your group's work process is critical to capitalizing on the stage with negligible disturbance. A CRM framework is just basically as great as the information that is added to it, so ensure you've carried out it with the genuine way your group cooperates in view of clients. Any other way, it will be trying to get purchase from your group, and you might observe that information isn't advancing into the framework. Keep away from those issues with a fastidious and smart execution process. You'll be happy you found an opportunity to get it done.

Tackling the Force of Client Audits and Tributes

In the present computerized age, online surveys and tributes assume an essential part in molding the standing and outcome of organizations. Shoppers intensely depend on the encounters shared by others to settle on informed choices. With the ascent of stages like Google Business Profile (previously called Google My Business), organizations presently have an integral asset available to them to exhibit their image and influence the worth of surveys and tributes. In this article, I will investigate the meaning of audits and tributes and the advantages of using Google My Business for your image.

Laying out Trust and Validity Surveys

Surveys and tributes act as friendly confirmation and fundamentally influence purchasers' confidence in a brand. Positive surveys and tributes go about as support from fulfilled clients, imparting trust in expected purchasers. At the point when possibilities see genuine individuals sharing their positive encounters, it fabricates trust and validity, making them bound to pick your business over rivals. Google Business Profile permits clients to leave surveys straightforwardly on your profile, giving you a stage to grandstand the positive criticism you get.

Affecting Purchasing Choices

Studies have shown that most buyers read surveys prior to pursuing a buy choice. Positive surveys and tributes can influence expected clients to pick your image, going about as powerful figures in their purchasing process. By effectively overseeing and empowering audits on Google Business Profile, you can impact the dynamic cycle in support of yourself, catching the consideration of possibilities and expanding your possibilities changing over them into faithful clients.

Further developed Neighborhood Search Perceivability

Google Business Profile (GBP) is a fundamental device for nearby website streamlining (Web optimization). Making and streamlining your GBP posting expands your possibilities showing up in nearby query items when clients are searching for items or administrations in your space. Positive surveys and high evaluations on your GBP profile can likewise help your perceivability as Google as audits are a strong positioning component in Google's pursuit calculation. The more sure audits you aggregate, the higher your possibilities positioning higher in neighborhood query items, prompting expanded openness and potential client commitment.

Client Criticism and Bits of knowledge

Audits and tributes are significant for likely clients and give priceless criticism and bits of knowledge to your business. Client criticism assists you with understanding what you are doing well and distinguishing regions for development. It permits you to instantly address any worries or issues, showing your obligation to consumer loyalty. By effectively captivating with surveys on Google Business Profile and answering both positive and negative criticism, you show straightforwardness and a veritable interest in your clients' encounters.

Building a Positive Internet based Standing

Your web-based standing can represent the deciding moment of your business. Google Business Profile gives a stage to fabricate a positive internet based standing by exhibiting your image's assets and your clients' positive encounters. By reliably gathering and advancing positive surveys, you can lay out a great web-based picture that draws in new clients and supports entrust with existing ones. Dealing with your GBP profile and answering surveys shows your obligation to client support and features your image's responsiveness.

Notwithstanding the various advantages of surveys and tributes, organizations frequently face difficulties with regards to requesting and getting input from their clients. How about we investigate a portion of these difficulties:

Hesitance to Leave Surveys: A few clients might wonder whether or not to leave audits or tributes, regardless of whether they had a positive encounter. They could have an uncertain outlook on the most proficient method to compose a survey or not focus on it. Beating this challenge expects organizations to proactively empower and teach their clients on the significance of audits and the most common way of leaving criticism.

Negative Input: While positive audits are profoundly alluring, organizations should likewise be ready for negative criticism. Negative surveys can be demoralizing and may affect the brand's standing. Be that as it may, moving toward negative criticism as a chance for improvement is vital. Answering quickly and expertly to negative audits can exhibit your obligation to consumer loyalty and grandstand your ability to address concerns.

Conflicting Survey Volume: Keeping a predictable progression of surveys can challenge. There might be periods where the quantity of surveys diminishes, making it challenging to grandstand a powerful and exceptional web-based standing. Organizations should carry out techniques to urge clients to leave surveys reliably, for example, email crusades, web-based entertainment updates, or motivations for leaving criticism.

Best Using Client Tributes

These tributes are genuine encounters shared by fulfilled clients, giving social verification of the quality and dependability of items or administrations. Client tributes can be utilized across different showcasing channels, including sites, online entertainment stages, and limited time materials, offering a strong underwriting of a brand's contributions. They give consolation and approval to likely clients, making it more straightforward for them to pursue informed choices and certainly pick the business. Whether through composed tributes, video tributes, or online surveys, utilizing client tributes is a powerful technique that can essentially impact purchaser discernments and drive business development.

Make It Simple for Them; Recollect that, They Are Occupied.

Request that their consent use it across all stages.

Send them the connection to your LinkedIn and Google accounts so they can post.

Give them the system you believe that they should expound on. Here is a model:

What were the principal challenges you were confronting when you connected?

How did our item/administration address or settle those difficulties?

What positive results or results have you encountered since utilizing our item/administration?

Could you suggest our item/administration to other people? Assuming this is the case, why?

These inquiries are intended to urge clients to give explicit subtleties and individual bits of knowledge about their experience, taking into consideration a convincing and bona fide tribute that features the item's or alternately administration's assets.

CHAPTER 8: FINANCIAL MANAGEMENT AND GROWTH

Monetary administration is pivotal for any business or individual looking for development. It includes different practices focused on successfully taking care of funds to accomplish objectives and cultivate development. Monetary administration is a unique field that adjusts to changing financial scenes and individual conditions. Its standards apply not exclusively to organizations yet additionally to individual budgets. Here are A few key perspectives include:

Planning: Making a monetary arrangement that frames pay and costs helps in distributing assets productively.

Speculation: Decisively putting overflow finances in adventures that yield returns adds to abundance gathering and business development.

Risk The board: Distinguishing and relieving monetary dangers through protection, enhancement, and possibility arranging shields against expected misfortunes.

Income The board: Checking and enhancing income guarantees there's sufficient liquidity to cover functional necessities and immediately jump all over development chances.

Obligation The executives: Capable getting and ideal reimbursement procedures can use obligation as a device for development without overburdening funds.

Monetary Detailing and Examination: Ordinary evaluation of budget reports helps in settling on informed choices, recognizing patterns, and making arrangements for what's in store. Fruitful monetary administration encourages solidness, works with extension, draws in financial backers, and empowers productive utilization of assets, at last adding to supported development and flourishing.

Long haul Arranging: Laying out long haul monetary objectives and coming up with systems to accomplish them gives guidance and motivation. Whether it's putting something aside for retirement, extending a business, or buying resources, it is fundamental to have a reasonable arrangement.

Cost Control: Checking and overseeing costs help in enhancing costs without compromising quality. This can include haggling more ideal arrangements with providers, working on functional proficiency, or embracing savvy advancements.

Monetary Innovation (Fintech): Embracing fintech arrangements like advanced installments, computerized bookkeeping, and simulated intelligence driven monetary examination devices smoothes out processes, upgrades exactness, and further develops navigation.

Charge Arranging: Understanding assessment regulations and executing procedures to limit charge liabilities is fundamental. This includes exploiting allowances, credits, and assessment proficient speculation choices.

Versatility and Adaptability: In the present quickly impacting world, being versatile to showcase changes and open to changing monetary methodologies is urgent for supported development and soundness.

Moral and Reasonable Works on: Integrating moral contemplations and supportability into monetary choices benefits society and the climate as well as resounds decidedly with partners, encouraging long haul trust and development.

Monetary administration is a constant interaction that includes evaluation, change, and vital navigation. Its application is fundamental, whether you're running a global partnership or overseeing individual budgets.

High level Monetary Preparation and Anticipating

High level monetary preparation and estimating are fundamental parts for organizations meaning to settle on informed choices, moderate dangers, and accomplish economical development. Here are a few key viewpoints:

Situation Investigation: Using progressed anticipating procedures includes evaluating numerous situations in view of different suspicions. This aids in figuring out expected results in various monetary conditions, empowering proactive anticipating vulnerabilities.

High level Demonstrating Procedures: Utilizing quantitative models, for example, Monte Carlo reproductions or relapse examination considers a more nuanced comprehension of likely future monetary results. These models assist in anticipating with changing out streams, surveying gambles, and enhancing systems.

Incorporated Monetary Preparation: Uniting different parts of monetary preparation, including planning, income gauging, and vital preparation, makes an exhaustive view that guides decision-production across divisions and upgrades by and large hierarchical execution.

Prescient Investigation: Utilizing authentic information and using prescient examination instruments can conjecture future patterns and ways of behaving. This guides in settling non-information driven choices, recognizing amazing open doors, and expecting difficulties before they emerge.

Capital Planning: High level monetary arranging includes complex strategies for assessing long haul speculation choices. Methods like Net Present Worth (NPV), Inward Pace of Return (IRR), or Chance Changed Return help in surveying the suitability and benefit of venture projects.

Constant Observing and Audit: Routinely returning to gauges and plans in light of continuous information and market changes is significant. This iterative cycle considers changes, guaranteeing plans stay lined up with advancing business conditions.

Responsiveness Investigation: This strategy includes changing key factors inside monetary models to survey their effect on results. It helps in understanding the awareness of projections to changes in economic situations, permitting organizations to plan possibilities.

Dynamic Gauging: Integrating ongoing information into determining models empowers a powerful perspective on monetary presentation. This approach gives more exact expectations by considering current market patterns and prompt changes, improving readiness in direction.

Vital Asset Allotment: High level monetary arranging includes enhancing the designation of assets, including capital, HR, and time, to boost productivity and benefit. This might include focusing on projects, redistributing financial plans, or rebuilding tasks for improved results.

Risk the board and Moderation: Arrangement ahead of time stresses a proactive way to deal with risk the executives. It implies recognizing expected chances, evaluating their effect, and creating systems to alleviate or move these dangers to protect the association's monetary wellbeing.

Stress Testing: Past conventional gauging, stress testing assesses how a business or monetary model performs under outrageous circumstances. This thorough examination helps in evaluating strength, guaranteeing the association can endure unfavorable situations.

Correspondence and Coordinated effort: Powerful monetary preparation and gauging require cooperation among divisions and compelling correspondence of monetary systems. This arrangement guarantees that everybody pursues shared objectives and adds to accomplishing the ideal results.

By incorporating these high level procedures into monetary preparation and estimating processes, organizations can expect market shifts, streamline asset assignment, and settle on essential choices that drive supported development and achievement.

Strategies for Raising Capital and Investment

As a singular looking to raise capital and make ventures, there are a few procedures you can consider:

Reserve funds and Planning: Begin by saving a piece of your pay consistently and making a financial plan that focuses on saving. This structures the establishment for any money growth strategy.

Rainy day account: Lay out a backup stash to cover startling costs. Having this security net guarantees you won't have to dunk into your interests in the event of crises.

Obligation The board: Pay off exorbitant interest obligations to work on your monetary wellbeing. Paying off past commitments permits you to let loose more assets for saving and effective financial planning.

Manager Supported Plans: Exploit business supported retirement plans like 401(k)s or annuity plans. Contribute to the point of profiting from business matches, as this is basically free cash towards your future.

Individual Retirement Records (IRAs): Think about opening an IRA, either conventional or Roth, to enhance your retirement investment funds. These records offer expense benefits and an assortment of speculation choices.

Differentiated Ventures: Investigate different speculation choices like stocks, securities, shared assets, or trade exchange reserves (ETFs). Expansion helps spread risk and possibly increment returns.

Land: Research land open doors like buying property or putting resources into Land Speculation Trusts (REITs) as a method for broadening your portfolio and possibly procure automated revenue.

Side Pay or Business venture: Consider producing extra pay through a side gig or beginning a private company. The additional pay can be directed towards speculations.

Training and Expertise Advancement: Constantly put resources into yourself by obtaining new abilities or instruction that could prompt higher pay potential. This can in a roundabout way add to your venture capacities.

Monetary Counselor Meeting: Look for direction from a monetary consultant to think up a customized venture methodology lined up with your monetary objectives and chance resilience.

Keep in mind, the way to effective financial planning is consistency, expansion, and a drawn out point of view. Begin little, remain informed, and steadily increment your ventures as your monetary circumstance permits.

Monetary administration is vital for any business or individual looking for development. It includes different practices focused on really taking care of funds to accomplish objectives and encourage development. A few key perspectives include:

Planning: Making a monetary arrangement that frames pay and costs helps in distributing assets productively.

Speculation: Decisively putting overflow supports in adventures that yield returns adds to abundance amassing and business extension.

Risk The board: Recognizing and alleviating monetary dangers through protection, broadening, and possibility arranging shields against expected mishaps.

Income The board: Checking and streamlining income guarantees there's sufficient liquidity to cover functional requirements and quickly jump all over development chances.

Obligation The executives: Capable getting and opportune reimbursement procedures can use obligation as a device for development without overburdening funds.

Monetary Detailing and Examination: Standard appraisal of budget summaries helps in pursuing informed choices, distinguishing patterns, and making arrangements for what's in store.

Fruitful monetary administration cultivates solidness, works with extension, draws in financial backers, and empowers productive utilization of assets, eventually adding to supported development and flourishing.

Monetary administration is a unique field that adjusts to changing financial scenes and individual conditions. Its standards apply not exclusively to organizations yet additionally to individual budgets. Here are a few extra focuses:

Long haul Arranging: Laying out long haul monetary objectives and coming up with systems to accomplish them gives guidance and inspiration. Whether it's putting something aside for retirement, extending a business, or buying resources, it is fundamental to have a reasonable arrangement.

Cost Control: Observing and overseeing costs help in streamlining costs without compromising quality. This can include haggling more ideal arrangements with providers, working on functional productivity, or taking on practical advances.

Monetary Innovation (Fintech): Embracing fintech arrangements like computerized installments, robotized bookkeeping, and artificial intelligence driven monetary investigation apparatuses smoothes out processes, upgrades exactness, and further develops navigation.

Charge Arranging: Understanding assessment regulations and carrying out methodologies to limit charge liabilities is indispensable. This includes exploiting allowances, credits, and expense proficient venture choices.

Versatility and Adaptability: In the present quickly impacting world, being versatile to showcase vacillations and open to changing monetary methodologies is significant for supported development and security.

Moral and Feasible Works on: Integrating moral contemplations and manageability into monetary choices benefits society and the climate as well as reverberates decidedly with partners, cultivating long haul trust and development.

Monetary administration is a consistent interaction that includes evaluation, change, and vital direction. Its application is fundamental, whether you're running a global company or overseeing individual budgets.

Advanced Financial Planning and Forecasting:

High level monetary preparation and anticipating are fundamental parts for organizations meaning to settle on informed choices, relieve gambles, and accomplish feasible development. Here are a few key viewpoints:

Situation Examination: Using progressed estimating methods includes surveying different situations in light of different presumptions. This aids in figuring out expected results in various financial conditions, empowering proactive anticipating vulnerabilities.

High level Demonstrating Methods: Utilizing quantitative models, for example, Monte Carlo reenactments or relapse examination takes into consideration a more nuanced comprehension of likely future monetary results. These models assist in anticipating with changing out streams, surveying gambles, and advancing methodologies.

Incorporated Monetary Preparation: Uniting different parts of monetary preparation, including planning, income estimating, and key preparation, makes an exhaustive view that guides decision-production across divisions and upgrades generally hierarchical execution.

Prescient Examination: Utilizing authentic information and using prescient investigation instruments can estimate future patterns and ways of behaving. This guides in pursuing information driven choices, distinguishing valuable open doors, and expecting difficulties before they emerge.

Capital Planning: High level monetary arranging includes modern strategies for assessing long haul venture choices. Procedures like Net Present Worth (NPV), Inner Pace of Return (IRR), or Hazard Changed Return help in evaluating the suitability and productivity of speculation projects.

Constant Observing and Survey: Consistently returning to conjectures and plans in view of continuous information and market changes is critical. This iterative cycle considers changes, guaranteeing plans stay lined up with developing business conditions.

By incorporating these high level monetary preparation and estimating procedures, organizations can acquire an upper hand, improve asset distribution, and adjust quickly to changing business sector elements, subsequently upgrading generally speaking monetary execution and supportability.

Awareness Examination: This procedure includes changing key factors inside monetary models to evaluate their effect on results. It helps in understanding the responsiveness of projections to changes in economic situations, permitting organizations to plan possibilities.

Dynamic Determining: Integrating ongoing information into estimating models empowers a powerful perspective on monetary exhibition. This approach gives more precise forecasts by considering current market patterns and prompt changes, improving readiness in navigation.

Key Asset Allotment: High level monetary arranging includes advancing the distribution of assets, including capital, HR, and time, to expand productivity and benefit. This might include focusing on projects, redistributing spending plans, or rebuilding tasks for improved results.

Risk The board and Moderation: Timely arrangement underlines a proactive way to deal with risk the executives. It implies distinguishing expected gambles, measuring their effect, and creating methodologies to moderate or move these dangers to shield the association's monetary wellbeing.

Stress Testing: Past customary estimating, stress testing assesses how a business or monetary model performs under outrageous circumstances. This thorough examination helps in evaluating flexibility, guaranteeing the association can endure unfavorable situations.

Correspondence and Coordinated effort: Compelling monetary preparation and gauging require cooperation among divisions and viable correspondence of monetary methodologies. This arrangement guarantees that everybody pursues shared objectives and adds to accomplishing the ideal results.

By incorporating these high level methods into monetary preparation and estimating processes, organizations can expect market shifts, enhance asset portions, and go with vital choices that drive supported development and achievement.

As a singular trying to raise capital and make speculations, there are a few techniques you can consider

Investment funds and Planning: Begin by saving a part of your pay routinely and making a spending plan that focuses on saving. This structures the establishment for any money growth strategy.

Secret stash: Lay out a rainy day account to cover surprising costs. Having this wellbeing net guarantees you won't have to plunge into your interests in the event of crises.

Obligation The board: Pay off exorbitant interest obligations to work on your monetary wellbeing. Paying off past commitments permits you to let loose more assets for saving and money management.

Manager Supported Plans: Exploit boss supported retirement plans like 401(k)s or annuity plans. Contribute to the point of profiting from business matches, as this is basically free cash towards your future.

Individual Retirement Records (IRAs): Think about opening an IRA, either conventional or Roth, to enhance your retirement investment funds. These records offer duty benefits and an assortment of venture choices.

Differentiated Speculations: Investigate different venture choices like stocks, securities, common assets, or trade exchange reserves (ETFs). Expansion helps spread risk and possibly increment returns.

Land: Explore land open doors like buying property or putting resources into Land Speculation Trusts (REITs) as a method for expanding your portfolio and possibly procure automated revenue.

Side Pay or Business venture: Consider producing extra pay through a second job or beginning a private company. The additional pay can be directed towards ventures.

Training and Expertise Improvement: Persistently put resources into yourself by getting new abilities or schooling that could prompt higher pay potential. This can in a roundabout way add to your speculation capacities.

Monetary Counselor Discussion: Look for direction from a monetary guide to think up a customized speculation technique lined up with your monetary objectives and hazard resistance.

Keep in mind, the way to fruitful money management is consistency, broadening, and a drawn out point of view. Begin little, remain informed, and steadily increment your ventures as your monetary circumstance permits.

Global Development and Multi cash Exchanges

Extending universally as an individual includes exploring multi-cash exchanges and taking into account different perspectives:

- Unfamiliar Trade The board: Comprehend trade rates and their effect on your funds. Consider utilizing multi-cash accounts or on the other hand benefits presented by banks or monetary foundations to proficiently oversee various monetary standards.
- Money Hazard Alleviation: Changes in return rates can affect the worth of your resources. Techniques like supporting or enhancing money possessions can assist with moderating these dangers.
- Worldwide Financial Administrations: Investigate banking choices that take special care of multi-cash exchanges, offering cutthroat trade rates, low expenses, and advantageous exchange methods.Some banks offer multi-money accounts that permit people to hold, make due, and move subsidies in different monetary forms. These records frequently give ideal trade rates and decreased expenses for worldwide exchanges, working on the most common way of dealing with numerous monetary standards

- Installment Stages and Fintech Arrangements: Utilize online installment stages that help multi-money exchanges. A few stages offer good rates and simplicity of transformation for global installments or buys.

- Charge Suggestions: Grasp the assessment ramifications of holding unfamiliar resources or acquiring pay in various monetary forms. Talk with charge counselors or experts to guarantee consistent with applicable duty laws.When managing multi-cash exchanges, people ought to know about the assessment ramifications of unfamiliar speculations or pay acquired in various monetary forms. Grasping duty arrangements between nations, detailing prerequisites, and potential expense liabilities is urgent to guarantee consistency

- Statistical surveying and Social Getting it: Prior to extending universally, lead exhaustive statistical surveying to comprehend the objective market's inclinations, guidelines, and social subtleties. This aids in fitting items or administrations successfully.

- Legitimate and Administrative Consistence: Know about worldwide exchange guidelines, import/trade regulations, and consistency prerequisites while managing various nations. Complying with these guidelines is fundamental to stay away from legitimate issues.

- Risk Appraisal: Survey the dangers related with worldwide extension, including political shakiness, monetary circumstances, and administrative changes. Foster alternate courses of action to moderate these dangers.

- Associations and Systems administration: Laying out associations or organizations in the objective nation can give significant bits of knowledge, backing, and potential open doors for smoother market section and development.

- Consistent Assessment and Variation: Routinely audit your global procedures, taking into account changing economic situations, financial vacillations, and client inclinations. Adjust your methodology on a case by case basis to remain serious.

- Extending globally requires cautious preparation, careful exploration, and a comprehension of the intricacies engaged with multi-money exchanges. Remain informed, look for master guidance when essential, and move toward worldwide extension decisively to amplify achievement..

- Online Installment Stages and Fintech Arrangements: Using on the web installment stages that help multi-money exchanges can smooth out global installments or buys. A few stages offer cutthroat trade rates, lower exchange expenses, and easy to use interfaces, making it more straightforward to go through with cross-line exchanges.

- Enhancement and Resource Designation: Broadening speculations across various monetary standards and geological areas can assist with spreading risk. By assigning resources across different monetary standards or global business sectors, people might possibly lessen the effect of cash changes on their general portfolio.

- Exchange and Financial Circumstances: Global extension requires a thorough comprehension of the monetary, political, and administrative scene of the objective nations. Factors, for example, economic deals, international soundness, expansion rates, and neighborhood economic situations assume a critical part in the outcome of worldwide endeavors.

- Innovation and Advancement: Utilizing innovation, for example, blockchain-based arrangements or fintech developments, can smooth out cross-line exchanges, lessen expenses, and upgrade straightforwardness in multi-cash exchanges.

- Social Variation and Limitation: Grasping social subtleties, customer conduct, and inclinations in various business sectors is basic. Adjusting items, administrations, or advertising systems to resound with neighborhood societies can significantly impact the outcome of worldwide extension endeavors.

- By taking into account these itemized parts of worldwide extension and multi-money exchanges, people can explore intricacies all the more really, limit gambles, and profit by open doors introduced by worldwide business sectors.

CHAPTER 9: SCALING AND MECHANIZATION

Scaling and mechanization are essential to the outcome of any internet based organizations. Scaling includes extending the span and effect of the business obliging development in clients. Computerization smoothes out processes, saving time and assets while guaranteeing productivity.

Scaling and computerization remain forever inseparable to impel an internet based business towards supportable development and improved proficiency.

While scaling an institute, it's vital to zero in on differentiating course contributions, upgrading mechanical abilities, and extending effort through essential promoting endeavors. This development plans to oblige a bigger crowd and meet the developing necessities of students.

In the mean time, mechanization assumes an essential part in streamlining different parts of the business tasks. Via mechanizing regulatory undertakings like enlistment processes, installment dealing with, and significant time and assets are monitored, permitting staff to zero in on additional basic undertakings. Moreover, carrying out computerized frameworks for customized encounters, criticism assortment, and support administrations can fundamentally improve client commitment and fulfillment.

The collaboration among scaling and mechanization isn't just about development; it's likewise about keeping up with quality and encouraging a customized learning climate. Adjusting these components guarantees that the business can develop reasonably without settling on the individualized and top notch encounters that purchasers anticipate. This harmonious connection among scaling and mechanization shapes the foundation of a fruitful web-based business in the present unique computerized scene.

Viable Reevaluating and Designation

Maintaining a business of any size is, indeed, a precarious business. On one hand, you maintain that you should do everything. It's just normal. As a business visionary, there's a decent opportunity that you developed your organization from the beginning, as you came. Normally, there's a piece of you that simply expects to be that on the off chance that something should be finished, you ought to adapt to the situation and do it.

A few of us likewise work under the conviction that, "Assuming you need something done well, you really want to do it without anyone else's help.

Yet, while this is just fine, the truth of the matter is that assuming you believe your organization should develop dramatically, you must realize when to give up. A long way from being an image of rout, having the option to rethink and delegate really is the indication of an incredible pioneer. Having an incredible group on your side permits you to scale your organization to a level that just wouldn't be imaginable to all alone.

Figuring out how to really reevaluate will let loose you from being required to play out each of the ordinary assignments all alone, permitting you rather to empty your significant investment into pursuing key choices, executing development methodologies, further developing cycles, improving the client experience, and different things that are critical for your organization's drawn out progress. Sounds promising?

We should investigate.

Chipping away at Your Business Rather than in It

I would rather not break it to you, however as business people, we're exposed to a revile

That revile? The need to do everything

Nearly 98% of business people guarantee that their greatest test they face is, 'doing everything themselves and not having sufficient opportunity.' This is a telling measurement, and features perhaps the main issue that we're confronting today: the scourge of attempting to do everything ourselves. Maybe nobody puts it better than Michael E. Gerber, business master and top of the line creator of the E-Fantasy Returned to. As Gerber said, "Most business visionaries come up in no time since you are working IN your business rather than ON your business.

"Right when you see that the defense behind your life isn't to serve your business, yet that the fundamental occupation of your business is to serve your life

"When you perceive that the reason for your life isn't to serve your business, yet that the basic role of your business is to serve your life, you can then go to chip away at your business, as opposed to in it, with a full comprehension of why it is totally important for you to do as such.

All around said

For business people, it's a significant achievement when you understand that besides the fact that you rethink can, however that you Ought to!

Not exclusively will assigning help to hold you back from wearing out, it'll likewise permit you to quit wasting your time, and begin zeroing in on significant level errands that will permit you to drive your organization forward.

Back in the previous days of my business, and as of recently, I had been doing various regulatory errands - things that a menial helper might have done.

It didn't seem like a lot from the start, however after some time how much work that was engaged with these undertakings and the quantity of hours that I was spending on them, started to add up. When I recruited a VA and started re-appropriating, it let me step back and on second thought center around developing my organization.

Advantages of Re-appropriating

Okay, so we've checked out at the fundamental advantage of appointing: letting loose you to zero in on running your organization. In this segment, we should see a few advantages that come from moving to provisional laborers - like specialists, menial helpers, and other telecommuters.

This is a genuine youngster in-a-sweets store second for you! There are bunches of pretty sweet rewards that will come once you begin reevaluating, for however long it's done really.

1. **Expands Your Proficiency:** While you're rethinking, you'll have the option to proficiently work undeniably more. Since you'll invest undeniably less energy on tedious errands, you'll have the option to zero in on other, more urgent things all things being equal. Furthermore, it can assist your whole organization with working all the more proficiently also. Enrolling outside help for errands that would somehow or another must have your group perform permits them to keep on zeroing in on their standard obligations, without being occupied by additional assignments.

2. **Can Address Magnificent Expense Reserve funds:** The incredible thing about rethinking is that you just get compensation for what you want. Rather than planning for extra full-time staff and ensuring you'll have sufficient work to keep them occupied, you can basically rethink errands depending upon the situation. At times, it can work out to be significantly more practical than employing another colleague.

3. **Will Mean Less Cerebral pains:** While full-time staff can be vital, in certain circumstances it's a good idea to reevaluate. Designating a provisional laborer will assist you with staying away from the finance and expense cerebral pains. All things considered, you simply pay them, send them a 1099 structure, and afterward illuminate

the IRS toward the end regarding the year. They'll be answerable for documenting their own assessments.

4. **Compels You to Refine Your Interaction:** This may not seem like an advantage, but rather accept me, it is. While you're employing a worker for hire to assume control over specific undertakings, you'll need to separate your cycles into obvious frameworks for them to follow; complete with anticipated results. This permits you to smooth out your cycles and will give you quantifiable outcomes that you can follow too. With any standard working method, the objective ought to be to make it very straightforward. As a matter of fact, it ought to be easy to the point that a 5-year-old could do. A more definite interaction will have a lower opportunity of slip-ups and a lot more limited expectation to learn and adapt too.

5. **Permits You to Take advantage of Extra Assets:** You might grasp the intricate details of beginning, running, and working a fruitful organization, yet what might be said about finance and duties? And the law? There are a few things that you probably won't be aware of, and don't want to drench yourself in. Assigning these undertakings or moving to other people, who are educated here will permit you to take advantage of and benefit from their ability. Presently, not all undertakings are made equivalent. There are a things that you'll need to forgo re-appropriating, and others that you ought to think about designating. Alright, presently how about we move along and see which assignments you ought to designate.

6. **Concluding Which Errands to Reevaluate or Delegate:** As per Gregg Landers, head of development the board at CBIZ MHM; a bookkeeping and business administrations supplier, the kind of undertakings that are best re-appropriated can be classified into three general classifications:

7. **Exceptionally talented ability:** This incorporates legitimate guides. Or on the other hand, you could consider recruiting a part time chief. This would permit you to profit from the skill of an old pro, without keeping them for all time on the finance. Exceptionally dreary assignments.

This incorporates things like accounting, information passage, stock, booking, and managerial undertakings that a VA could do.

8. Particular information.

Different times, it could be valuable to move to somebody with expert information. For instance, you should consider having a virtual entertainment expert make an arrangement, and afterward meet with them at regular intervals to examine the procedure - while having a lower-paid worker for hire carry out the actual technique. Presently a fair warning. Before you make a plunge recklessly and begin re-appropriating, it's critical to ensure you're doing it for the right reasons. For example, it's not commonly smart to reevaluate occupations essentially in light of the fact that you detest them.

Many pioneers will presumably be thinking," AHA, I will re-appropriate deals since I could do without them," yet in all actuality, the best strategy is to re-appropriate while doing so will give you the most worth. Likewise, any region where a definitive effect is durable, for example, employing choices, is a region where you ought to continue cautiously with regards to designating - particularly in the event that you're a private company.

Numerous different assignments, however, can without much of a stretch be designated. Here is a gander at a few particularly normal undertakings that numerous business visionaries are picking to designate:

Accounting: Accounting is one assignment that entrepreneurs regularly disregard. However, without a reasonable and exact record of the books, you'll struggle with running your organization. Precise records are crucial for guaranteeing the soundness of your business and estimating the return for capital invested of various procedures. By re-appropriating this occupation to a clerk, you'll have the option to guarantee that you have precise and exceptional data that you want to keep on course and pursue significant choices. Furthermore, it's reasonable!

Finance: Finance is like accounting, and numerous accountants can do both. Nothing can cause you problems quicker than not paying the perfect proportion of duties. Staying aware of the consistent changes in government, state, and neighborhood expenses can be a bad dream. Help yourself out: reevaluate your finances and inhale simpler!

Web-based Entertainment Promoting

Web-based entertainment promoting and effort are frequently failed to be remembered by independent companies. With such countless additional major problems to be made due, things that aren't up front will generally drop off the radar. This is sad, taking into account a greater part of the present promotion is done on the web. Employing a specialist to create, screen, and deal with your web-based entertainment showcasing could be a commendable and practical speculation for your organization

Content Promoting

Like online entertainment showcasing, content advertising additionally matters. In the event that you're an online business, it's particularly essential to guarantee that you have a strong technique to attract new, significant guests to your site. You can effectively re-appropriate this work to an accomplished author who has insight in happy administration.

With each new representative or provisional laborer, there's continuously going to be somewhat of an expectation to learn and adapt. This doesn't be guaranteed to imply that you committed an error or recruited some unacceptable individual to get everything done. It takes anybody a couple of days to change. After the underlying round of input, they ought to be significantly more adjusted on the cycle and your assumptions. They'll proceed to improve, and you'll progressively have additional opportunity to zero in on different things.

Re-appropriating and assigning errands and occupations in your organization may be troublesome, and right away, you might feel that you're surrendering some proportion of control. However, it's vital to understand that eventually, reevaluating will give you more command over your business, and not less. Offloading redundant or master level assignments to another person will permit you to pull together your endeavors and consider where it makes the biggest difference - developing your organization.

Carrying out, Promoting and Deals Computerization

Carrying out promoting and dealing with computerization can altogether smooth out cycles and lift effectiveness in your business. Here is a bit by bit guide:

1. Set Clear Targets: Characterize your objectives for robotization: Would you say you are meaning to increment lead age, further develop change rates, or smooth out correspondence?

2. Pick the Right Apparatuses: Research and select robotization programming or stages that line up with your business needs. Choices include:

- Advertising Computerization Instruments (e.g., HubSpot, Marketo, Mailchimp)
- Client Relationship The board (CRM) Programming (e.g., Salesforce, Zoho CRM)
- Deals Computerization Instruments (e.g., Effort, Salesloft)

3. Coordinate Frameworks: Guarantee consistent joining between your picked mechanization apparatuses and existing frameworks (e.g., site, CRM, email stage).

4. Distinguish Work processes and Cycles: Map out your promoting and deals work processes. Characterize key touchpoints from lead age to transformation and then some.

5. Make Designated Missions: Foster designated promoting efforts in light of client division and purchaser personas. Mechanize email advertising, virtual entertainment booking, and content conveyance.

6. Lead Sustaining: Carry out robotized work processes for lead supporting. Use dribble crusades, customized content, and set off reactions in view of client conduct.

7. Deals Computerization: Set up computerization for deals processes, including lead scoring, task, and subsequent meet-ups. Use CRM programming to follow connections, focus on leads, and smooth out the deals pipeline.

8. Personalization and Customization: Use mechanization to customize messages, offers, and collaborations in view of client information and conduct.

9. Testing and Advancement: Constantly test and advance your mechanized missions. Examine measurements, A/B test various methodologies, and refine procedures for improved results.

10. Preparing and Reception: Train your group on utilizing the computerization devices really. Energize reception and offer continuous help for investigating and streamlining.

11. Consistence and Checking: Guarantee consistency with information insurance guidelines (e.g., GDPR, CCPA). Consistently screen and review computerized cycles to keep up with consistency.

12. Assess and Change: Routinely survey the presentation of your mechanized showcasing and deals endeavors. Change methodologies in light of results and changing economic situations.

13. Criticism Circle: Assemble input from clients and inner partners to refine and further develop mechanization systems.

14. Scale and Grow: As your business develops, scales and grows your robotization endeavors to cover new channels, sections, or cycles.

15. Remain Refreshed: Stay up to date with headways in mechanization innovation and advertising/deals patterns. Adjust your techniques as needed to remain cutthroat.

Executing showcasing and deals robotization requires key preparation, ceaseless observing, and a pledge to adjusting and further developing cycles after some time. Begin with clear objectives and step by step grow and refine your robotization endeavors for most extreme adequacy

Scalable Technologies And System

1. The Power of Scalable Technologies: In the present high speed advanced world, organizations are continually looking for ways of remaining in front of the opposition and drive development. One key component that can have a huge effect in accomplishing this objective is the utilization of versatile advancements. Versatile innovations allude to the devices, frameworks, and cycles that can without much of a stretch adjust and extend as a business develops, considering

consistent adaptability and expanded proficiency. In this part, we will investigate the different manners by which versatile advances can enable organizations and drive their development.

2. Smoothed out Tasks: One of the essential benefits of versatile advancements is their capacity to smooth out tasks. By carrying out adaptable programming arrangements and frameworks, organizations can robotize dreary undertakings, lessen manual blunders, and work on by and large proficiency. For instance, cloud-based client relationship the board (CRM) stages empower organizations to incorporate client information, computerize work processes, and give ongoing bits of knowledge, prompting better client encounters and smoothed out deals processes.

3. Adaptability and Flexibility: Versatile advancements offer adaptability and flexibility, permitting organizations to rapidly answer and adjust to changing business sector requests. For example, distributed computing empowers organizations to increase their processing assets or down depending on the situation, without the requirement for critical equipment ventures. This adaptability guarantees that organizations can productively deal with unexpected spikes sought after or change their tasks during lean periods, eventually working on cost-adequacy and consumer loyalty.

4. Upgraded Coordinated effort and Correspondence: Powerful coordinated effort and correspondence are indispensable for any business' prosperity. Adaptable advancements give the important apparatuses and stages to work with consistent joint effort across groups, divisions, and, surprisingly, geological areas. For instance, project board programming with coordinated correspondence highlights permits groups to team up continuously, share records, and track progress, prompting further developed efficiency and quicker independent direction.

5. Cost Investment funds: Versatile advancements can likewise bring about tremendous expense reserve funds for organizations. By utilizing cloud-based arrangements, organizations can keep away from forthright foundation costs, like buying and keeping up with servers. Moreover, versatile innovations empower organizations to pay just for the assets they use, staying away from superfluous costs during times of low interest. These expense reserve funds can then be reinvested in different region of the business, like promoting, innovative work, or ability securing.

6. Contextual investigation: Airbnb: A perfect representation of an organization that utilized versatile innovations for dramatic development is Airbnb. In its beginning phases, Airbnb confronted the test of scaling its foundation to oblige expanding client interest. By taking on distributed computing and using amazon Web administrations (AWS), Airbnb had the option to scale its framework quickly, guaranteeing a consistent client experience in any event, during top booking periods. This versatility assumed a pivotal part in Airbnb's prosperity, permitting it to develop from a little startup to a worldwide neighborliness goliath.

7. Ways to use Adaptable Advances: To successfully use adaptable advancements for business development, think about the accompanying tips:

- Distinguish and focus on regions of your business that can profit from versatility, for example, client support, tasks, or promoting.

- Research and select adaptable programming arrangements that line up with your business objectives and prerequisites.

- Routinely assess and advance your versatile innovations to guarantee they keep on gathering your developing necessities.

- Put resources into preparing and advancement to guarantee your group can completely use the abilities of adaptable innovations.

- remain refreshed with the most recent headways and patterns in versatile advances to stay serious in your industry.

Versatile innovations have turned into a trendy expression in the present quickly developing computerized scene. As organizations endeavor to stay aware of changing client requests and market drifts, the requirement for adaptable advances has never been more significant. In this part, we will jump further into what versatile advances are, their definition, and the advantages they proposition to organizations.

Meaning of Adaptable Advancements:

Versatile innovations allude to the capacity of a framework, application, or foundation to deal with a rising responsibility without forfeiting execution or client experience. In more straightforward terms, versatile advances are intended to develop and adjust consistently as the requests on them increment. This adaptability can be accomplished through different means, for example, flat or vertical scaling, distributed computing, or the utilization of disseminated frameworks.

Benefits of Scalable Technologies:

Carrying out adaptable advancements can carry a few advantages to organizations, empowering them to remain dexterous, cutthroat, and receptive to showcase changes. A few key advantages include:

1. Adaptability: Versatile innovations permit organizations to oblige development and variances popular without any problem. Whether it's an unexpected flood in site traffic, expanded information capacity prerequisites, or extending client base, versatile innovations can easily increase or down to meet these changes.

2. Cost reserve funds: Adaptable advancements assist organizations with improving their asset designation and decrease pointless expenses. With versatile framework, organizations can stay away from overprovisioning assets, paying just for what they need, and keeping away from costly equipment speculations.

3. Improved execution: Versatile advances guarantee that framework execution stays steady, much under weighty responsibilities. By conveying the heap across different servers or assets, adaptable advances can forestall bottlenecks and lulls, bringing about better client experience and consumer loyalty.

4. Further developed unwavering quality: Adaptable advances frequently utilize overt repetitiveness and shortcoming lenient structures, guaranteeing high accessibility and limiting the gamble of framework disappointments. By disseminating responsibility across various servers, regardless of whether one server goes down, the framework can flawlessly divert traffic to other accessible assets.

Instances of Versatile Advances:

A few advancements and approaches empower versatility in various parts of business tasks..Coming up next are several models:

- Distributed computing: Cloud stages like Amazon Web Administrations (AWS), Microsoft Purplish blue, or research Cloud give versatile framework and administrations, permitting organizations to scale their processing assets in view of interest.

- Content Conveyance Organizations (CDNs): CDNs disseminate site content across various servers situated in various geographic areas. By reserving and conveying content from the closest server to the client, CDNs further develop site execution and handle high traffic proficiently.

- Data set Sharding: Sharding includes evenly dividing a data set into more modest, more sensible shards. This takes into consideration circulated information capacity and further develops data set execution as the responsibility increments.

Ways to execute Versatile Advances:

To take advantage of versatile innovations, organizations ought to think about the accompanying tips:

- Plan for versatility all along: Integrate versatility into the engineering and plan of your situation and applications right all along. This will save time and exertion in the future while scaling becomes important.

- Screen and examine execution: Routinely screen and dissect framework execution to recognize expected bottlenecks or regions that require improvement. This will help in proactively tending to adaptability challenges.

- Embrace mechanization: Influence robotization devices and cycles to proficiently oversee and scale your foundation. Robotization works on asset provisioning, sending, and observing, considering speedy scaling when required.

- Contextual investigations: Various organizations have utilized adaptable innovations to make amazing development and progress. For example, Netflix uses an adaptable cloud framework to stream motion pictures and Television programs to a great many clients around the world. By scaling their foundation in light of interest, Netflix guarantees continuous streaming and an amazing client experience.

Likewise, Airbnb, a famous internet based commercial center for transient rentals, depends on versatile innovations to deal with a gigantic volume of appointments and requests. By scaling their frameworks, Airbnb guarantees that their foundation stays responsive and accessible, in any event, during top booking seasons.

The Job of Versatile Advances in Business Development

Versatile advances assume a significant part in driving business development in the present speedy computerized scene. These advances enable organizations to adjust and grow their tasks flawlessly, permitting them to satisfy the rising needs of clients and remain serious on the lookout. In this segment, we will investigate the different manners by which versatile advances add to business development, giving models, tips, and contextual analyses to outline their adequacy.

1. Fulfilling Client Needs: One of the essential advantages of adaptable innovations is their capacity to deal with developing client requests. As organizations grow, they frequently face difficulties in overseeing expanded client requests, requests, and information. Adaptable advancements, for example, distributed computing and client relationship the executives (CRM) frameworks, empower organizations to productively scale their tasks. For instance, a cloud-based online business stage can without much of a stretch handle a flood in site traffic during top shopping seasons, guaranteeing a consistent shopping experience for clients.

2. upgrading Functional proficiency: Versatile advancements smooth out business processes, bringing about better functional effectiveness. Mechanization devices, like mechanical interaction robotization (RPA) or AI calculations, can computerize dreary errands, diminishing human mistakes and opening up significant assets. By carrying out adaptable advancements,

organizations can improve their work processes, limit manual mediations, and accomplish higher efficiency levels. For example, a strategies organization can use versatile innovations to mechanize stock administration, request following, and conveyance booking, bringing about quicker and more precise tasks.

3. extending Business sector reach: Adaptable innovations empower organizations to extend their market venture and tap into new client fragments. With the coming of computerized showcasing and web-based entertainment stages, organizations can use adaptable advances to target explicit socioeconomics and draw in with likely clients. For instance, a little internet clothing store can utilize versatile innovations like site design improvement (Web optimization) and designated publicizing to contact a worldwide crowd, growing its client base past geological limits.

4. Working with information driven Navigation: Information assumes a crucial part in driving business development, and versatile innovations furnish organizations with the instruments to gather, examine, and influence information really. By carrying out adaptable information examination arrangements, organizations can acquire significant experiences into client conduct, market patterns, and functional execution. These experiences empower informed navigation, permitting organizations to recognize open doors, streamline techniques, and drive development. For example, a product as-a-administration (SaaS) organization can utilize versatile innovations to break down client information and distinguish designs, prompting item upgrades and expanded consumer loyalty.

Distinguishing Versatile Advancements for Your Business

Advancements that can be utilized in your business with regards to developing your business, critical to put resources into versatile innovations can uphold your development and adjust to evolving needs. These advancements assist with smoothing out tasks as well as empower you to immediately take advantage of new chances and remain in front of the opposition. Notwithstanding, with a plenty of choices accessible, distinguishing the right versatile innovations for your business can dismay. In this part, we will investigate a few critical variables to consider and give models, tips, and contextual investigations to assist you with pursuing informed choices.

1. Evaluate your business needs: Prior to jumping into the universe of adaptable advances, it's fundamental to survey your business needs completely. Consider the trouble spots you as of now face, the regions where you expect development, and the particular objectives you need to accomplish. For instance, in the event that you're a quickly growing web based business organization, you might require a strong stock administration framework that can deal with a high volume of orders and coordinate with your current stages. By understanding your requirements, you can distinguish innovations that line up with your business targets.

2. Research accessible advances: When you have a reasonable comprehension of your business needs, now is the right time to explore the accessible advancements on the lookout. Search for arrangements that offer adaptability, adaptability, and consistent mix with your current frameworks. For example, distributed computing stages like Amazon Web Administrations (AWS) and Microsoft Purplish blue give adaptable framework and administrations that can oblige your business development. These stages permit you to increase or down in view of interest, guaranteeing ideal execution and cost-effectiveness.

3. Look for proposals and contextual investigations: Feel free to suggestions from industry companions or specialists who have effectively carried out versatile advances. Their encounters can give important bits of knowledge and assist you with staying away from possible entanglements. Furthermore, contextual analyses of organizations like yours can offer motivation and direction on the advancements that have yielded positive outcomes. For instance, assuming that you're a SaaS startup, you could find contextual investigations of organizations that have successfully used microservices engineering to scale their applications.

4. Think about the drawn out influence: Versatile innovations shouldn't just address your prompt necessities yet additionally can possibly uphold your drawn out development. Assess how an innovation can develop with your business and oblige future extension. This could include considering factors like versatility, adaptability, merchant support, and the capacity to coordinate with arising advances. For example, on the off chance that you're a retail business wanting to venture into worldwide business sectors, picking an internet business stage that upholds various dialects, monetary standards, and duty guidelines is significant for long haul versatility.

5. Test and repeat: Before completely focusing on a versatile innovation, leading exhaustive testing and evaluation is fitting. Carry out a pilot project or a proof-of-idea to evaluate how the innovation

Tips for Successful Implementation:

- Direct exhaustive examination and assess different versatile innovations prior to going with a choice.

- Include your IT group and partners in the dynamic cycle to guarantee arrangement with your association's objectives and targets.

- Routinely survey and enhance your versatile foundation to stay aware of developing necessities and headways in innovation.

- - Think about versatility as far as framework as well as far as programming advancement rehearses, like particular and reusable code.

Carrying out adaptable advances is critical for organizations looking for supportable development in the present computerized scene. By following accepted procedures, anticipating future development, utilizing distributed computing, embracing containerization, and executing robotized observing and scaling instruments, associations can guarantee their foundation can deal with expanding requests while keeping up with ideal execution and client experience.

Best Practices and Contemplations - Versatile Advances: Tech Strengthening: Utilizing Adaptable Innovations for Business Development

Best Practices and Contemplations - Versatile Advances: Tech Strengthening: Utilizing Adaptable Innovations for Business Development

Effective Organizations Utilizing Versatile Advances

1. Amazon: One of the most noticeable instances of a business utilizing versatile innovations is Amazon. With its gigantic internet based retail stage, Amazon has effectively utilized versatile advances to deal with the tremendous volume of exchanges and information. By carrying out distributed computing and versatile framework, Amazon guarantees that its foundation remains exceptionally accessible, in any event, during busy times like the huge shopping day after Thanksgiving or The online Christmas sales extravaganza. This versatility has permitted the organization to develop quickly and become one of the world's biggest web-based retailers.

2. Netflix: Netflix is one more perfect representation of a business that has bridled the force of versatile innovations. With its real time feature, Netflix conveys top notch video content to a large number of clients around the world. By utilizing versatile innovations, for example, cloud-based framework and content conveyance organizations (CDNs), Netflix can deal with the enormous interest for its administrations without forfeiting execution. This versatility has empowered Netflix to extend its client base and reform the manner in which individuals consume media.

3. Airbnb: As a main internet based commercial center for momentary convenience rentals, Airbnb depends vigorously on versatile innovations to help its foundation. By using distributed computing and circulated frameworks, Airbnb can deal with the rising number of appointments and guarantee a consistent encounter for the two hosts and visitors. Versatility plays had a critical impact in Airbnb's development, permitting the organization to grow its administrations universally and upset the conventional inn industry.

Ways to use Adaptable Advancements:

1. Embrace distributed computing: Cloud-based administrations give the adaptability and versatility expected to help business development. By moving your framework and applications to the cloud, you can without much of a stretch scale assets up or down in view of interest.

2. Use containerization: Containerization advancements like Docker take into account the effective sending and scaling of utilizations. Holders give a segregated climate to applications, making it simpler to oversee and scale them depending on the situation.

3. Execute a microservices design: Separating your applications into more modest, free administrations empowers better versatility and adaptability. With a microservices engineering, you can scale individual parts of your application freely, guaranteeing ideal asset use.

4. Influence content conveyance organizations (CDNs): CDNs assist with circulating substance topographically, lessening idleness and further developing execution. By storing and conveying content from servers nearer to the end-clients, CDNs can deal with high traffic stacks and further develop the client experience. Different tips include:

- Remain refreshed with the most recent patterns and headways in versatile advancements to distinguish potential open doors for development and development.

- Direct intensive examination and investigation to comprehend the particular necessities and difficulties of your industry prior to executing versatile arrangements.

- Team up with innovation accomplices or specialists who can give direction and backing in executing adaptable advancements successfully.

- Persistently screen and assess the presentation of your versatile answers for distinguish regions for development and advancement.

- Cultivate a culture of development inside your association, empowering representatives to investigate and try different things with versatile innovations to drive business development.

Conquering Difficulties in Scaling Advances for Business Development

Defeating Difficulties Conquering these difficulties and scaling Advances that can be utilized in your business. Scaling innovations for business development can be an invigorating yet testing attempt. As organizations extend and request increments, it becomes essential to guarantee that the innovation framework can uphold the developing necessities. Nonetheless, there are a few hindrances that associations might look en route. In this part, we will investigate a few normal difficulties experienced while scaling advances and give tips and models on the most proficient method to conquer them.

1. Versatility constraints: One of the essential difficulties in scaling advancements is managing adaptability impediments. As the business develops, the current innovation foundation might battle to deal with the expanded burden. For example, a site that was at first intended to help a couple hundred clients each day might encounter execution issues when the client base extends to thousands or millions. To beat this test, associations can utilize strategies, for example, load adjusting, reserving, and utilizing cloud-based administrations to appropriate the responsibility effectively and guarantee ideal execution.

2. Information the board and capacity: One more obstacle in scaling advancements is overseeing and putting away enormous volumes of information. As business tasks grow, how much information is produced and handled increments altogether. Customary data sets might battle to deal with the steadily developing information prerequisites. Executing versatile and strong information the board framework, for example, a disseminated data set or a cloud-based capacity arrangement, can assist organizations with defeating this test. For instance, organizations like Airbnb and Netflix have effectively utilized cloud-based capacity answers for handle their enormous information necessities.

3. Security and protection concerns: With development comes the requirement for elevated safety efforts to safeguard delicate information. Scaling advances can open organizations to new security dangers and weaknesses. It is urgent to execute hearty security conventions to protect against possible dangers. This might incorporate utilizing encryption strategies, executing secure access controls, and routinely checking and examining frameworks for any likely breaks. Contextual investigations like the Equifax information break act as a wake up call of the significance of focusing on security while scaling innovations.

4. Ability securing and preparing: Scaling advancements require talented experts who can oversee and keep up with the framework really. Notwithstanding, finding and employing the right ability can be testing, particularly in a serious work market. Associations ought to put resources into ability procurement procedures, like organizations with instructive establishments or offering preparing projects to existing workers. By supporting a gifted labor force, organizations can beat the test of finding and holding qualified experts.

6. Computerized reasoning (simulated intelligence) and AI (ML): Quite possibly the main pattern in adaptable advances is the rising reception of simulated intelligence and ML. These innovations can possibly upset different businesses via robotizing processes, further developing productivity, and giving significant experiences. For instance, computer based intelligence controlled chatbots can deal with client questions, decreasing the requirement for human mediation and improving client experience. ML calculations can dissect huge measures of information to distinguish examples and make forecasts, empowering organizations to go with information driven choices.

7. Web of Things (WOT): The WOT alludes to the organization of interconnected gadgets that can gather and trade information. This innovation has massive potential for adaptability, as it permits organizations to accumulate constant information from different sources and pursue informed choices. For example, in the assembling business, IoT sensors can screen gear execution, recognize abnormalities, and trigger upkeep alarms, limiting margin time and upgrading creation processes.

8. Blockchain Innovation: Blockchain has acquired huge consideration because of its capability to change different areas, including finance, production network the executives, and medical care. Its decentralized and straightforward nature guarantees information respectability and security, making it an optimal innovation for adaptable arrangements. For instance, blockchain can be utilized to make secure and recognizable inventory chains, empowering organizations to follow the development of merchandise and guarantee realness.

9. Edge Registering: With the coming of the Web of Things and the rising interest for ongoing information handling, edge figuring has arisen as a unique advantage.

Harnessing the Potential of Scalable Technologies for Sustainable Business Growth

In the present quickly developing advanced scene, organizations are continually looking for ways of remaining in front of the opposition and accomplish maintainable development. Versatile advancements have arisen as a distinct advantage in such manner, offering organizations the capacity to consistently adjust and extend their tasks. All through this blog, we have investigated the different parts of utilizing versatile advances for business development, and in this closing segment, we will sum up the critical focal points and give a few last experiences.

1. Embrace the Cloud: Distributed computing has altered the manner in which organizations work and scale. By utilizing cloud-based arrangements, organizations can dispose of the requirement for expensive foundation speculations and effectively scale their activities depending on the situation. For instance, stages like Amazon Web Administrations (AWS) and Microsoft Purplish blue give a large number of versatile administrations that can be customized to meet explicit business needs.

2. Computerize Cycles: Adaptable advances offer organizations the chance to mechanize different cycles, decreasing manual blunders, saving time, and expanding efficiency. For example, executing mechanical interaction mechanization (RPA) can smooth out dull errands, permitting workers to zero in on more worth added exercises. This further develops effectiveness as well as empowers organizations to scale without the requirement for extra HR.

3. Execute Coordinated Advancement: Deft philosophies have acquired notoriety lately because of their capacity to proficiently convey projects quicker and the sky is the limit from there. By taking on a coordinated methodology, organizations can separate complex undertakings into more modest, sensible errands, considering persistent improvement and transformation. For instance, utilizing nimble programming improvement practices can empower organizations to rapidly answer changing business sector requests and scale their items or administrations appropriately.

4. Influence Information Examination: Adaptable advances furnish organizations with admittance to immense measures of information. By utilizing information examination instruments, organizations can acquire significant bits of knowledge into client conduct, market patterns, and functional productivity. For example, utilizing AI calculations can assist organizations with distinguishing examples and settle on information driven choices, at last prompting reasonable development.

Contextual analysis: Netflix

Netflix is a perfect representation of an organization that has effectively tackled the capability of versatile innovations for business development. By utilizing distributed computing, Netflix had the option to scale its streaming stage worldwide, arriving at a huge number of endorsers without the requirement for costly framework speculations. Moreover, their utilization of information examination has permitted them to customize suggestions and further develop client experience, bringing about expanded client maintenance and income development.

Ways to tackle Adaptable Advances:

- Begin little and continuous scale: It is crucial for testing and approving versatile innovations on a more limited size prior to carrying out them across the whole association. This approach takes into account changes and calibrating without taking a chance with significant disturbances to business tasks.

- Cultivate a culture of development: To completely saddle the capability of versatile innovations, organizations ought to support a culture of development and consistent learning. This includes giving representatives the essential preparation and assets to embrace new advances and investigate creative arrangements.

- Remain informed and adjust: Innovation is continually developing, and organizations need to remain refreshed on the most recent patterns and headways. By keeping a heartbeat on industry improvements, organizations can adjust their procedures and influence arising versatile innovations to keep an upper hand.

All in all, adaptable advances have the ability to alter business tasks and drive economical development. By embracing distributed computing, robotizing processes, executing nimble improvement techniques, and utilizing information examination, organizations can open their maximum capacity and remain on the ball. With the right methodology and outlook, versatile advancements can turn into an impetus for progress in the present computerized age.

CHAPTER10: FUTURE- SEALING YOUR WEB-BASED BUSINESS

In the event that your business endured a significant shot, might it at any point get by? With the present quick changes in the two business sectors and innovation, that is an inquiry a great deal of organizations are posing. What it comes down to is this: Is your business future-verification?

While future-sealing a business could seem like something for big business partnerships and worldwide industry, any association of any size can apply the essential standards of future-sealing to build its possibility of enduring a significant emergency fundamentally.

Future-sealing your business implies planning for the unforeseen — any conceivable difficulty or danger that could emerge. Obviously, that is a difficult task. How would you get ready for in a real sense anything?

Rather than making explicit strides against a particular danger, future-confirmation organizations execute a progression of best practices intended to help any effective business adjust and get by, addressing future requirements and industry improvements regardless of what lies ahead.

Adjusting to Arising Advancements and Patterns

Variety TV opened up to buyers only quite a while back. The primary cell appeared only a long time back. Our cells have had the option to interface with the Web for only 20 years. Furthermore, just within the past 2 years, portable Web access has passed work area Web access - we're online on our telephones more than we are on our PCs. That is a ton of mechanical change in an extremely short measure of time. Obviously, organizations need to adjust to keep up. In the event that you didn't grow up around innovation like the millennial age, how might you embrace the most recent innovation patterns to effectively assist with maintaining your business more?

The key, similarly as with numerous things throughout everyday life, is keeping a receptive outlook and being tenacious. As a little organization, you likely don't have the advantage of a tech group to stay up with the latest on every one of the state of the art improvements in your industry. Fortunately you needn't bother with a tech group. You can stay aware of the significant advances through industry distributions so you know what's applicable to your business. You additionally don't need to be out on the extreme front line (in spite of the fact that you surely can assume you need to); you simply have to follow the significant patterns so you don't fall behind.

New innovations are intended to be not difficult to utilize and dominate. You could try and end up partaking during the time spent learning. In particular, the most recent innovation patterns can really improve your business.

Instructions to Utilize Innovation Patterns to Work on Your Business

"To remain cutthroat, private companies need to take on and integrate online innovation into their regular business activities," says Seong Ohm, senior VP of product business administrations at Sam's Club. These are only a portion of the manners in which innovation can work on your business:

- Quicker Finance: Finance applications can facilitate checks, put aside direct installments, and even electronically document charges. With the space of a committed clerk or finance organization, PC projects can now deal with practically all of your finance needs with next to zero contribution from you.

- Better Web-based Perceivability: Each business ought to have a site, yet that site is just basically as great as individuals who track down it. Computerized advertising tech can improve your internet based presence and assist your clients with finding you.

- Easier Accounting: Nobody likes keeping the books or doing their assessments. Current tech can assist you with monitoring every one of the fundamental records, solicitations, derivations, and consumptions to make each of the somewhat less agonizing. You may not require a bookkeeper! For instance, Enliven can monitor the entirety of your funds and help you produce and track solicitations.

- Dealing with Your Plan for the day: With a private venture, there are dependably 1,000,000 things that need to finish. Efficiency applications like Todoist can assist you with monitoring the main priority and when - you can likewise adjust them to your schedules and different projects so everything refreshes simultaneously!

- The "It" Element: Customers are more mechanically sharp than any time in recent memory and they notice when organizations have obsolete sites, installment handling frameworks, and different advancements. They generally need the freshest and best tech (look at the line at the Apple store at whatever point another iPhone emerges), so staying aware of tech patterns shows your clients that you comprehend what they need.

Instructions to Really Stay aware of The Most recent Innovation Patterns

Since innovation changes so rapidly, it may very well be overwhelming to attempt to stay up with the latest things. Adaptability and a receptive outlook, nonetheless, will work well for your business.

"I've tracked down that numerous entrepreneurs, whenever they've tracked down systems that work for them, will generally dawdle on new innovation," says Brian Carter, creator and President of The Carter Gathering. "They can erroneously accept that since one technique has consistently worked previously, it will continuously work from here on out."

The issue with this "on the off chance that it ain't penniless, don't fix it" That's what mentality is assuming your rivals are as of now utilizing new innovation, you might be abandoned. This is especially valid for online retailers. Neglecting to stay aware of the most recent innovation patterns, whether it's product updates or site usefulness or another part of your item or administration, can mean disaster for your business. As an entrepreneur, you've proactively demonstrated the way that you can be adaptable and master new abilities really. Those characteristics are exactly what you really want to deal with mechanical advances.

To assist your business with flourishing, the initial step is teaching yourself about new innovation. You can track down free assets as diaries, sites, and sites, outfitted explicitly to important new innovation in your field. Finding the distribution which addresses you about tech improvements gives you a leaping off point, and acclimates you with tech language and accessible items. This will provide you with a feeling of what choices are out there and how different organizations are exploiting them.

One more method for staying aware of the most recent innovation patterns is to take stock of what innovation you use and endeavor to smooth out your ongoing tech needs. In the event that you have a few distinct projects for various parts of your business - for instance, finance and bookkeeping - check whether there are redundancies. Research whether there is a later, high level program, application, or tech improvement that can total numerous requirements into one interaction.

At the point when you catch wind of an up and coming innovation or program being utilized in your industry, do some exploration on it! Figure out what makes it not the same as more established contributions and what other entrepreneurs are talking about it. For instance, spas might exploit an application or program that permits clients to book arrangements on the web. Moving organizations might utilize programming to effectively deal with their courses more. Take as much time as is needed, clarify some pressing issues, and conclude whether the new innovation is ideal for your business.

In the event that you're not happy hopping all alone to explore the most recent patterns, it's alright to request help! You might realize somebody who's innovatively slanted, or you could take a class on the web or at a nearby school to gain proficiency with a portion of the nuts and bolts and get some kind of foothold.

Top 5 Tech Fundamentals

There are more choices for programming and new innovation out there than you can shake a stick at, so it very well might be overpowering to attempt to overhaul everything simultaneously. On the off chance that you're pondering where to begin, these tech basics will help basically any private company.

- Cloud Joint efforts: "The cloud" gets thrown around a ton nowadays, however basically it implies putting away information so that you and your group can get to it from any gadget. That implies you can team up with your sellers, representatives, and different gatherings without sending around a Disc or a glimmer drive or some other actual stockpiling gadget. Data put away in the Cloud refreshes right away, implying that everybody in question approaches the most forward-thinking information.Do you have an email account? That is a sort of Distributed storage - you can get to your messages from any PC. You can utilize Google Drive and different kinds of Distributed storage to share inner archives, team up on activities, from there, the sky's the limit. Programs like Asana and Headquarters are an extraordinary method for monitoring the things you're dealing with across the board.

- Portable Installments: First it was cash, then, at that point, it was charge cards, and presently it is the right time to begin tolerating versatile installments. Apple Pay, Google Pay, and other versatile installment choices make installment and email invoicing in a real sense as simple as the press of a button. Your clients like the accommodation and you'll like the programmed recordkeeping.

- Shrewd Gadgets: A cell phone or tablet can be utilized for data, course, gathering installment, stock, charging, timekeeping, and then some, all in a hurry. You can utilize it to browse your messages and monitor the information your business is producing, regardless of where you are. You really want a savvy gadget to deal with your business.

- Online protection: Verizon announced that 63,000 information breaks influenced the world's greatest organizations last year and little organizations are similarly powerless.

Retail location burglary (computerized robbery from taken charge card numbers) is a typical worry for clients, as is burglary of their own data. Network safety frameworks and projects can safeguard your clients' personalities and funds and construct trust. On the off chance that you manage especially delicate data, it could be advantageous to employ a specialist to come in and ensure your projects and PCs are pretty much as secure as could truly be anticipated.

- Web-based Entertainment Applications: Virtual entertainment applications and stages are free for clients, so you have assets readily available to find, speak with, and market to clients. This is an introduction while heading to involve virtual entertainment for your private venture. Most virtual entertainment stages are instinctive and easy to use, so they're a simple way for you to connect with your clients.

The Priority Variation For The present Independent company

Some of the time, the most ideal way to deal with adjusting to the most recent innovation patterns is to approach it slowly and carefully. This is that urgent initial step. To the extent that innovation goes, there's one thing that you totally can't be without: a responsive site. Most US grown-ups (up to 64 percent) own some sort of "shrewd" gadget, so having the option to arrive at clients in a hurry is non-debatable.

You may be considering what a responsive site is. Basically, a responsive site is a site which adjusts the design for ideal review on more modest cell phones, for example, PDAs or tablets. In the event that your site isn't responsive, then it tends to be provoking for your clients to see or use on their telephones or tablets. Best case scenario, this implies a baffling encounter for your clients. Even from a pessimistic standpoint, it implies you lost a deal or client to a contender with a superior versatile web insight. In the event that you want to fabricate a site without any preparation or change your own, here's an asset to assist you with those means.

"I would portray an inability to have a dynamic site in the equivalent way as an inability to redesign from a pony and truck to a vehicle in the period of Henry Passage," Walker says. "You'll make due for a short time frame but at last you'll be bankrupt as all of your opponents are tremendous and little run you down."

Try not to allow your rivals to run you down! Adjust and advance to keep pace.

In conclusion

The most recent innovation patterns can make your occupation simpler and will likewise show your clients that your business is present day and developing. Stay aware of what's hot in your industry and put forth the attempt to coordinate the innovation that is best for your business.

Exploring Administrative CHANGES AND Information Security

Information security is undeniably something other than the security and insurance of individual information. The main thing really is the means by which associations are utilizing that individual information. Associations need to handle individual information in a moral and lawful way. That could mean not barraging clients with undesirable SMS advertising messages however it could likewise mean just not offering individual data to outsiders without the client's assent. It doesn't imply that advertising is currently taboo under information security regulations yet it implies that associations should be straightforward about what individual information they are catching and how it will be utilized. Numerous affiliations see the basic risks of advanced attacks and data breaks anyway disregard to comprehend what else is generally anticipated to safeguard what is implied as the "privileges and and opportunities of people".

As the business scene turns out to be progressively perplexing and worldwide, organizations are confronted with a bunch of administrative changes that present the two open doors and difficulties.

Understanding the potential gamble these administrative movements convey, and planning for them, is necessary to business versatility. A tabletop practice approach can be instrumental in evaluating and dealing with these dangers.

Tabletop practices are organized, situation driven exercises that give a protected and controlled climate for a business to assess its reaction and recuperation procedures in case of administrative changes. This approach guarantees the organization's preparation to change its functional methods and can assist with distinguishing likely areas of hazard.

We should investigate how we can use this methodology with regards to changing administrative scenes.

1. Recognizing the Administrative Changes

The most important phase in any tabletop practice is to recognize the progressions in guidelines that might actually influence the business. Changes can go from little acclimations to industry-explicit principles to expansive changes in worldwide economic accords. It is crucial for keep up to date with the ongoing news and impending official improvements that could influence your plan of action or area.

2. Characterizing the Tabletop Exercise Situation

When the administrative changes are recognized, a speculative situation ought to be created in light of these changes. For example, in the event that another information security guideline is normal, the situation could include an information break that tests the organization's consistence with the new regulations.

3. Running the Tabletop Exercise

This stage includes assembling every single pertinent partner, including the board, lawful, consistence, and activities groups. They will manage the speculative situation to distinguish how the business will answer the administrative change. This exercise will uncover expected shortcomings and weaknesses inside the current construction that could raise the gamble.

4. Survey and Examination

Following the activity, a careful survey ought to be directed to recognize the illustrations took in, the holes in systems, and the regions that need reinforcing. This survey interaction can likewise assist the organization with planning an exhaustive gamble the board procedure.

Administrative changes convey the gamble of serious monetary punishments and reputational harm while perhaps not suitably made due. For example, the presentation of GDPR (General Information Assurance Guideline) in 2018 prompted organizations overall scrambling to guarantee they were agreeable. Organizations that neglected to adjust were hit with powerful fines.

We should dive further into a few potential administrative changes that could elevate business gambles:

1. Changes in Natural Guidelines

As worldwide center movements towards maintainability, changes in ecological guidelines are turning out to be progressively normal. Organizations need to evaluate their natural impression and change in a like manner. In the event that is not supervised well, these progressions could prompt monetary dangers due to resistance fines and reputational risk from negative public discernment.

2.. Information Protection and Network safety Guidelines

In the time of digitization, information security and network protection have become the dominant focal point. The rising severity of information insurance guidelines overall presents a critical gamble. Without the appropriate frameworks and conventions set up, organizations can have to deal with strong damages and lose buyer trust.

3. Exchange Guidelines: Exchange guidelines, like taxes, shares, and bans, can essentially influence organizations with worldwide activities or supply chains. Inability to adjust to these

progressions could bring about inflated costs, inventory network interruptions, and possibly stressed associations with unfamiliar accomplices.

4. . Monetary Detailing Guidelines: Changes in monetary detailing principles, similar to the progress from GAAP to IFRS, can require significant alterations to an organization's monetary administration and revealing cycles. Rebelliousness with these principles can bring about monetary punishments and harm financial backer relations.

5.Work Regulations and Guidelines: Work regulations and guidelines are another region that can fundamentally affect organizations. Changes might influence wages, working hours, wellbeing and security norms, or even remote work arrangements. Resistance can prompt suit, monetary punishments, and harm to an organization's standing.

The significance of a tabletop approach in exploring these administrative changes can't be overemphasized. It not just distinguishes expected shortcomings and weaknesses in an organization's reaction system yet in addition gives a way towards successful gamble relief and the executives.

We ought to summarize the major advances again:

- Recognize the administrative changes and expected influence on your business.
- Characterize a speculative situation in view of these changes.
- Run the tabletop practice including every one of the pertinent partners.

- Survey and dissect the results to track down areas of progress.

A proactive way to deal with administrative change in the executives is imperative in the present high speed and steadily changing business climate. This is where tabletop practices come in. By giving a controlled, sans risk climate to evaluate expected situations and reactions, tabletop practices furnish organizations with the instruments they need to explore through administrative changes effectively and limit related gambles.

Besides, associations should cultivate a culture of constant learning and flexibility. Along these lines, representatives at all levels can add to take a chance with the executives endeavors. Keep in mind, exploring administrative changes isn't exclusively the obligation of the consistency group however an aggregate exertion including the whole association.

For what reason is information security significant?

Organizations that neglect to safeguard individual information and consent to information security guidelines aren't simply taking a chance with monetary punishments. They additionally risk functional failures, mediation by controllers and above all, extremely durable loss of buyer trust.

Information insurance controllers might implement compulsory reviews, demand admittance to documentation and proof or even command that an association quits handling individual information.

Ten moves toward a successful information security program

1. Choose an Information Insurance Official

2. Keep an individual information register

3. Tell reason and look for assent

4. Answer when people get some information about their own information

5. Implement security instruments

6. Install information protection into your frameworks, cycles and administrations

7. Advise information breaks

8. Oversee outsiders

9. Safeguard individual information while moving abroad

10. Convey your information assurance strategies, practices and cycle.

Building a Maintainable and Versatile Web-based Endeavor

Maintainability isn't simply a popular expression or a pattern. It is a need and a chance for organizations that need to flourish in the 21st 100 years. As per a new overview by McKinsey, 42% of chiefs hope to put maintainability at the focal point of their new organizations' incentive, and 70 percent accept that supportability will mean a lot to their clients in the following five years.

Yet, what's the significance here for organizations? Also, how might they incorporate it into their center procedure, activities, and culture? In this article we will investigate a portion of the vital standards and practices that can assist organizations with turning out to be more manageable and versatile despite natural, social, and monetary difficulties.

Maintainability isn't just about lessening natural effects. It is additionally about making positive incentives for all partners, including clients, representatives, providers, networks, and financial backers. This implies embracing a roundabout and helpful plan of action that limits squander, expands asset effectiveness, and improves social prosperity.

A roundabout and helpful plan of action depends on three primary points of support:

- Planning items and administrations that are sturdy, reusable, repairable, and recyclable, and that utilizes inexhaustible or reused materials whenever the situation allows.

- Improving the utilization of assets and energy all through the item life cycle, from obtaining to assembling to dissemination to utilization to end-of-life.

- Recovering regular and social capital by reestablishing debased biological systems, supporting neighborhood networks, and adding to worldwide objectives like the UN Feasible Improvement Objectives.

A portion of the advantages of taking on a round and supportive plan of action are:

1. Diminished expenses and dangers related with asset shortage, instability, and guideline.

2. Expanded incomes and piece of the pie from offering inventive arrangements that address client issues and inclinations for maintainability.

3. Upgraded standing and trust from showing authority and obligation in tending to worldwide difficulties.- Further developed representative commitment and maintenance from encouraging a culture of direction and development.

Be that as it may, changing to a round and supportive plan of action is difficult. It requires a major change in outlook, technique, and capacities. Organizations need to reevaluate their incentive, their worth chain, their worth organization, and their worth creation process. They additionally need to team up with different partners, like providers, clients, contenders, controllers, NGOs, and the scholarly world, to co-make arrangements that benefit the entire framework.

One method for beginning this excursion is to gain from the accepted procedures of manageability of new businesses. These are organizations that have assembled their plans of action around supportability all along. They have utilized innovation, imagination, and joint effort to settle the absolute most squeezing issues on the planet. A few instances of such new businesses are:

- . Allbirds: A footwear organization that utilizes normal materials like fleece, eucalyptus, and sugarcane to cause agreeable and in vogue shoes that have a lower ecological impression than traditional ones.

- .Ecosia: A web search tool that uses its benefits to establish trees all over the planet. Ecosia has established north of 150 million trees up until this point, which assist with combating environmental change, reestablishing biodiversity, and backing neighborhood networks.

- Circle: A stage that empowers customers to purchase ordinary items from driving brands in reusable bundling that is gathered, cleaned, topped off, and conveyed once more. Circle plans to dispense with single-utilize plastic waste and make a round economy for shopper products.

These are only a portion of the instances of how supportability can be a wellspring of development and upper hand for organizations.

Dominating advertising procedures to construct and grow a web-based business resembles setting out on a thrilling excursion where you're continually learning new things, adjusting to changes, and tracking down imaginative ways of associating with individuals.

Everything without a doubt revolves around being interested and remaining open to novel thoughts on the grounds that the computerized world is continuously evolving. Thus, being adaptable and evaluating new methodologies assists your business with remaining ahead in the game.

Something major is keeping your clients blissful. It resembles building fellowships; you need to comprehend what they like, what they need, and afterward offer them something that genuinely helps them.

Gracious, and information! Like having a mystery map lets you know where to go. Utilizing information helps settle on more astute choices, such as sorting out who may be keen on the thing you're advertising.

Obviously, there are difficulties en route. In any case, very much like throughout everyday life, remaining solid when circumstances become difficult, gaining from botches, and not surrendering are vital to pushing ahead.

Likewise, it's anything but a performance trip! Interfacing with others, sharing thoughts, and cooperating can make the excursion significantly really astonishing and fulfilling.

Eventually, dominating promoting methodologies for your web-based business is a blend of innovativeness, flexibility, and a ton of heart. Embracing change, being available to new kinships, and continuously endeavoring to offer some benefit will assist your business with sparkling in the always developing advanced world!

Survey PAGE

Dear Peruser,

I trust this message believes that you are well. We profoundly esteem the suppositions and encounters of our clients since they guide us in constantly working on our items/administrations.

Your new connection/buy/insight with us implies a ton, and we would incredibly see the value in a snapshot of your chance to share your considerations. Your criticism is pivotal in assisting us with better comprehension of your necessities and how we can serve you far superior.

Could you benevolently think about leaving us a survey? Your genuine criticism assists us with improving as well as helps different clients in settling on informed choices

You can leave your audit and in the event that you experienced any difficulties or have ideas for development, kindly go ahead and share them. Your experiences are significant to us!

Much thanks for being a piece of our loved ones. We truly value your help and anticipate hearing from you.

Warm respects,

Melissa M. Backes

www.ingramcontent.com/pod-product-compliance
Lightning Source LLC
Chambersburg PA
CBHW080925260726
48661CB00010B/3808